YOUTH, EMPIRE AND SOCIETY

Youth, Empire and Society

British Youth Movements, 1883 – 1940

JOHN SPRINGHALL

CROOM HELM LONDON
ARCHON BOOKS, HAMDEN, CONNECTICUT

© 1977 John Springhall
Croom Helm Ltd, 2-10 St John's Road, London SW11

ISBN 0-85664-102-2

First published in the United States of America 1977
as an ARCHON BOOK, an imprint of
The Shoe String Press, Inc., Hamden, Ct.

Library of Congress Cataloging in Publication Data

Springhall, John
    Youth, Empire, and society.

    Includes bibliographical references and index.
    1. Youth movement – Great Britain – History.
I. Title.
HN19.S75   369.4'0941   76-47688
ISBN 0-208-01640-6

Printed in Great Britain
by Redwood Burn Ltd, Trowbridge and Esher

CONTENTS

ILLUSTRATIONS

SOURCES

The sources of the illustrations are: Plate 1, *The Bailie*, 20 September 1893; Plate 2, Anon., *A History of the Glasgow Battalion* (Glasgow, 1891), p. 123; Plate 3, Dr. Thomas Fraser, New University of Ulster; Plate 4, Enfield Scout Association; Plate 5, Mrs. P. B. Nevill; Plate 6(a), David Grace; Plate 6(b), Army Cadet Force Association; Plate 7, Church Lads' Brigade; Plate 8, *Punch*, 1 September 1909; Plate 9, Woodcraft Folk Headquarters; Plate 10, Church Lads' Brigade.

ABBREVIATIONS

BB	Boys' Brigade
BLB	Boys' Life Brigade
BM	British Museum
BNCA	British National Cadet Association
CCTA	Central Council of the County Territorial Army Associations
CLB	Church Lads' Brigade
CETS	Church of England Temperance Society
COS	Charity Organization Society
JLB	Jewish Lads' Brigade
LDCLB	London Diocesan Church Lads' Brigade
OWC	Order of Woodcraft Chivalry
PP	Parliamentary Papers
PRO	Public Record Office
RACS	Royal Arsenal Co-Operative Society
YMCA	Young Men's Christian Association
YWCA	Young Women's Christian Association

SCOUT COMMISSIONERS

ELLES, Sir Edmund, (1848-1934)

Chief Scout Commissioner, 1909-1922.
Born in 1848, married the daughter of a general, educated privately, then Royal Military Academy, Woolwich. Entered Royal Artillery in 1867, became Colonel in 1891 and a Major-General in 1900. Elles saw service in numerous of the 'little wars' of the Empire, including the Looshai expedition (1871-1872), Egypt (1882), Hazara expedition (1888), and the Indian Frontier (1897). Elles commanded the Mohmand expeditionary force and was in charge of the Peshawur District of India from 1895 to 1900. He was made Adjutant-General in 1900, and became a Military Member of the Governor-General's Council in India from 1901 to 1905. He retired with the rank of Lieutenant-General in 1908 and became Chairman of the Surrey County Territorial Force Association from 1907 to 1927, during which time he was also a Surrey Alderman. Elles sat on the National Council of the Territorials and was a member of the executive committees of both the National Service League and the Boy Scout Governing Council before 1914. Sir Francis Vane cites Elles as remarking that his only object in joining the Scouts was, 'for the purpose of getting recruits for the Territorials.' See Vane, *'Agin the Governments'* (London, 1929), p. 210.

CRUM, Major F. M., (1872-1955)

Chief Scout's Commissioner for Scotland, 1913-1929.
Born in 1872 and educated at Eton College and the Royal Military College (now Academy). Joined the King's Royal Rifle Corps in 1893 and served in the Boer War with the Mounted Infantry, where he was badly wounded and held captive until the relief of Pretoria in 1900. After this he was sent to India but in 1908 he broke down from overwork during the hot weather while running a Mounted Infantry School near Poonah. Being restless and energetic, in 1911 he decided to resign from the Army and devote his life to some form of public service, having already worked with the Boy Scouts in Stirling during his sickleave from India. Baden-Powell's response was: 'Good man, I chucked the Army for Scouting — it's much nicer. Hope he will do it.' After the

removal of the incompetent Marquess holding the post, Crum was appointed Scout Commissioner for Scotland. A strong imperialist with marked anti-socialist views, Crum was a dedicated youth worker eager to encourage co-operation between the various youth movements. He founded the Stirling Boys' Club in 1928, was made an Honorary Captain in the Boys' Brigade and a Deputy Lieutenant of the County. In the 1930s he became Chairman of the Stirling Juvenile Advisory Committee and in the late 1940s sat on the Scottish Council of Juvenile Organizations. On his death-bed he expressed a wish that the 'great Commander-in-Chief' would say to him, 'Fall out, Crum'. See Crum, *With Riflemen, Scouts and Snipers, 1914-1919* (Oxford, 1921); *With the Mounted Infantry in South Africa* (London, 1903); *The Youth Problem* (Stirling, 1942); *Memoirs of a Rifleman Scout* (Edinburgh, 1950). Major Crum's private papers are in the National Library of Scotland, Edinburgh.

MEATH, 12th Earl of, (1841-1928)

Scout Commissioner for Ireland, 1911-1928
Reginald Brabazon, 12th Earl of Meath, sat in the House of Lords as Baron Chaworth. Educated at Eton, in the 1860s he served as a diplomat at British embassies in Frankfurt, Berlin and Paris. But a promising diplomatic career in the Foreign Office was brought to an abrupt end in 1873 when Meath was posted to Athens and his wife's parents objected; thus he embarked upon a career of public philanthropy that was to span several decades. As well as his more charitable work, such as the Brabazon Employment Society, Meath also founded such voluntary organizations as: the Lads' Drill Association (1899-1906), and the Duty and Discipline Movement (1910-1919); while also finding time to serve on the executive of the National Service Leage and the Boy Scout Council. He is best remembered, perhaps, for setting up the Empire Day Movement, which he ran himself from 1903 to 1913, when a committee took over some of the work. He was appointed to the Boy Scout Council in December 1909 and made a Scout Commissioner for Ireland, where he owned a large estate, in 1911. With Baden-Powell he shared a social-imperialist belief that, 'the Darwinian theory of the survival of the fittest applies to nations as well as to individuals.' (See Meath, 'What the Boy Scout Movement may do for Britain', *The Windsor Magazine* (Dec., 1909), p. 56.) Meath enthusiastically endorsed Scout training as one more method for preventing the 'moral decay' of the British Empire. During the early 1920s, together with Lord Powerscourt,

he was instrumental in guiding the Boy Scouts through a difficult transition in Irish political life. Meath was made a member of the Irish Free State Senate, an Irish Privy Councillor and a Lord Lieutenant of Dublin. He published many books on social and imperial questions and two volumes of anecdotal autobiography. See J. O. Springhall, 'Lord Meath, Youth, and Empire' in *The Journal of Contemporary History*, Vol. 5, No. 4 (1970), pp. 97-111.

PREFACE

'Because the apologetics of youth movements are callow, their arguments crude, and their practices puerile,' wrote Leslie Paul self-depreciatingly in 1951, 'they are dismissed or ignored by scholars.' This book was originally intended as a contribution towards remedying that deficiency by placing the major British youth movements — Scouts, Brigades, Cadets — in the historical situation common to such voluntary organizations of the late-nineteenth and early-twentieth centuries. Not unexpectedly, since beginning my research some five years ago, I have encountered others with a similar intent, often much better equipped to write such a history than myself. I am, therefore, especially grateful to the following for being generous enough to share with me both their interest in and their hard won knowledge of this field: Paul Wilkinson, David Prynn, John Gillis, John Hodgson and Sidney Bunt. Much more work still remains to be done, however, on the 'view from below' — the meaning and experience of being in a youth movement to its participants — before the historian can come anywhere near estimating the social and cultural importance of youth movements. A more detailed investigation of individual movements than I have been able to provide here would also be a potentially fruitful source of historical inquiry, particularly at the regional and local levels.

I was greatly assisted in gathering material for this historical survey by being allowed to consult the archives held by the youth movements themselves, and I would like to thank the following for making these records available, often at some inconvenience to themselves: Miss M. D. Ellis, Senior Records Assistant, Boys' Brigade, London; Harold Wyld, Press Secretary and J. A. Allen, Relationships Secretary, Scout Association; G. A. Taylor and K. R. Buxton, Church Lads' Brigade; W. F. L. Newcombe, General Secretary, Army Cadet Force Association. In Glasgow, I was able to consult material on the Boys' Brigade through the courtesy of John M. Leggat, Glasgow Battalion Secretary and Captain Douglas G. H. Rolland of the 1st Glasgow Company. The following owners of private papers allowed me access to and gave me permission to quote from material in their possession: the late P. B. Nevill, Dr Ben Ridge, L. R. Moody, Alexander Martin, the present Lord Baden-Powell and his cousin, Francis Baden-Powell. In addition the following members and ex-members of youth movements were good enough to grant me taped interviews which are held in the History Film and Sound Archive of the New University of Ulster: the late P. B. Nevill, P. L. Purnell, G. G. Wilkinson, the late George Clayton (Scout Movement); T. Sharman, W. H. McVicker, Hugh McCallum, Fordyce Guy, A. E. Hinckins, E. A. Sweetman, E. J. Berkelmans (Boys' Brigade); A. J. Ormiston, J. Veysey, the late A. G. Bradford (Church Lads' Brigade); M. Robins (Jewish Lads' Brigade).

I should mention that parts of my 1968 Sussex University doctoral thesis on 'Youth and Empire' have been incorporated into this work, which rather belatedly recalls a particular debt to my supervisor and long-time mentor, Ranajit Guha, Reader in the School of African and Asian Studies at Sussex. I am also indebted to the following scholars, historians and friends for performing one of the essential penances of academic life in offering their careful comments and suggestions on various chapters in draft: Richard Price, Brian Harrison, Raphael Samuel, Keith Nield, Iain Hutchinson, Norman Vance, Martin Clark and Hugh Cunningham. I would also like to extend my thanks to the editors of the series in which this work appears, Professor J. F. C. Harrison and Stephen Yeo of the University of Sussex, for their close reading of the text; although all errors of fact and interpretation are, naturally, my own responsibility. It would have been difficult to complete the research necessary for this history while teaching in Northern Ireland without frequent visits to London and the British Museum: these were made possible by research grants and study leave from the New University of Ulster and an award from the Twenty Seven Foundation. I would also like to acknowledge the help of the staff of this University's inter-library loan service in providing an invaluable research aid. Without the secretarial skills of Miss Helen Agnew and Mrs Tita Gatrell a presentable typescript would not have been completed.

(In the absence of a dedication, I would like to thank my parents for tolerating my presence during lengthy stays in London.)

John Springhall
Portstewart, Northern Ireland
June 1976

INTRODUCTION

A youth movement or organization will be identified, for the purposes of this study, by its willingness to admit unlimited numbers of children, adolescents, and young adults, with the aim of propagating some sort of code of living. It should also encourage the participation of its youthful members as leaders and organizers, allow for the possibility of competing for awards and badges, and provide them with a specific identity or status in the form of a uniform.[1] Such a definition is useful, if for no other reason than that it conveniently restricts our attention — with the exception of the tiny woodcraft groups — to the mass, uniformed British youth movements selected here. It excludes youth clubs, the St. John's Ambulance Brigade, the YMCA and the Young Conservatives because, on the basis of the above characteristics, they do not constitute youth movements. Either they do not aim at comprehensiveness in membership or training, or they lack an explicit ideological framework, or they do not include a sufficient degree of youth involvement in leadership and organization.

To ask how many adults there are even today who have at some time or other in their lives been involved with youth movements, which constantly recruit new members in each generation, is to attempt an estimate of both their historical significance and potential influence in British society. At least *one adult in three* has belonged, however briefly, to the Boy Scouts or Girl Guides, while nearly *three out of five* men admitted when interviewed recently to belonging to one or more uniformed groups when young.[2] If numbers count in history, then one wonders how far the thirteen million or so who have passed through the Scouts and Guides since their inception, or the two million the Boys' Brigade claim to have sent out into the world, have been influenced in their general outlook by the training they have received. At the least, the impact of uniformed youth movements on the pattern of social and cultural behaviour in the twentieth century must have been considerable.

Youth movements do not claim the rather solemn attention of the historian simply because of the many thousands of boys and young men who have enlisted as members of such organizations. Over the past century, they have also functioned as extremely sensitive barometers of shifts in public and governmental attitudes towards the military in British society.[3] In addition, youth movements acted as indicators of

the general demographic, cultural and economic conditions conducive
to the recognition and institutionalization of adolescence that were
just beginning to come into existence around the turn of the century.[4]
But above all, they demonstrate with great clarity the sense of release
from suffocating urban squalor or dull, repetitive manual labour that the
ordinary boy discovered in the open air life of the annual camp or the
weekend excursion into the countryside.[5] If this aspect of youth
movements may receive insufficient attention hereinafter, I would
certainly not wish to deny its importance for their successful appeal to
the young. One of the crucial historical issues posed by youth movements as they have developed in Britain, however, is whether or not they
are best characterized by a 'hegemonic' relationship between leaders
and led, or whether they can be seen with equal validity as rungs on
the ladder of mobility to higher social status. A third possibility considered here is that there is no real or inherent contradiction between
the exercise of 'hegemony' and such opportunities for rising within the
social hierarchy as were provided for by a voluntary organization.

In general, the last decades of the nineteenth century and the first
of the twentieth — which saw the arrival of all the major British youth
movements — were a period of increasing economic and social uncertainty in Britain. The hopes and fears of an apprehensive middle class
struggling to consolidate its position against what were perceived as
threats both at home and from abroad were a characteristic elements
of this period. While industrial competition from America and Germany
undermined the fabric of business confidence, the expansion of German
naval power was widely viewed as a serious threat to the sea routes
on which the security of Britain's imperial possessions depended. At
home, the expanding influence of socialism, the growing strength of
organized labour and the gradual evolution of the Labour Party, threatened an intensification of class conflict. After the virtual collapse of
the New Unionism in the 1890s, this led to an employers' counter-
attack, confirmed by exaggerated middle-class fears of more openly
aggressive forms of working-class militancy.[6] The disastrous South
African war which followed, in revealing both the poor physical condition of the recruits and the inefficiency of their military commanders,
did little to inspire confidence in Britain's ability to maintain her Empire
intact. The British middle class, therefore, felt themselves to be menaced
on two sides: by the socialist enemy within from the mid-1880s and by
the German enemy without from at least the mid-1900s. This combination of internal and external threats to their own and the Empire's
ultimate survival led to a renewed cultural and social emphasis being

placed by the ruling élites on the question of cementing national unity.
A task which was seen as being more or less synonymous with the
problem of establishing the hegemony of the dominant ideology over
the rising generation.[7]

The second half of the nineteenth century also saw the 'national-
ization' of a wide variety of leisure activities marketed by churches
and chapels which were not available to the same extent in earlier
periods, such as the Christian Endeavour Societies, the Bands of Hope
and the Pleasant Sunday Afternoon Movement. If there is, in any one
period, a common context for voluntary organizations as such, this is
one of the specific settings around which the emergence of youth movements can be understood.[8] In this situation, with the Churches seeking
to retain the illusion of exercising a supervisory role over a rootless,
urban population, agencies were developed under middle-class control
to penetrate and organize the leisure of working-class adolescents.
Thus youth movements evolved at a time when they appeared to offer
an antidote to what could be seen, in a self-fulfilling way, as increasing
signs of juvenile restlessness. Consequently, the rapid growth of the new
youth movements, from the 1890s onwards, affected the increase in
anxiety about delinquency and had a marked effect on police enforce-
ment of new moral standards, leading to a rising rate of arrests for
certain non-indictable categories of juvenile crimes.[9]

The Boys' Brigade parading on the streets of Glasgow or the drilling
of working-class cadets in the quad of Toynbee Hall, demonstrated
that the discipline of school-room and work-place could be healthily
reinforced by voluntary youth movements:

> The habits of order, discipline and good conduct inculcated could
> not fail to beneficially affect [the cadets'] characters at an age
> when most susceptible to good or evil influences, training them to
> become loyal, manly and self-respecting members of society.[10]

If by the late 1900s, the 'cycle of anxiety' over delinquency had
declined, Scouting's over-riding concern at an official level with imperial
defence and racial survival supplanted earlier religious and moral
justifications for the mobilization of the young in uniformed youth
movements:

> We must all be bricks in the wall of that great edifice — the British
> Empire — and we must be careful that we do not let our differences
> of opinion on politics or other questions grow so strong as to divide

us, [exhorted Baden-Powell] we must still sticl shoulder to shoulder
as Britons if we want to keep our present position among the nations.[11]

Youth movements were, for the most part, developed as instruments
for the reinforcement of social conformity. They provided just such
institutional expression as was required to safe-guard 'legitimate'
middle-class interests while, at the same time, making sufficient pro-
visions for working-class leisure. They were formed during a period in
which the young found themselves increasingly becoming socialized
into national moulds by a committed middle class that took its *welt-
anschauung* from various permutations of militant Evangelical Christianity, public-school 'manliness', militarism and imperialism. What made
the young particularly vulnerable to social conditioning around the turn
of the century was their growing isolation and protection from adult
status; a privilege once confined to the upper and middle classes but which
was now beginning to filter down slowly to other levels of society.[12]
The 'invention' of adolescence as an age-defined social cohort further
segregated the young, as well as creating a 'social problem' whose
solution invariably became the provision of adult-supervised leisure
pursuits:

> The Church Lads' Brigade is getting hold of the lads at a critical
> period of their lives, [claimed a leaflet of the 1890s] and when it
> is so difficult to keep them within the control of those who are
> willing to teach them and encourage them to do their duty.[13]

Fear and self-interest had as much to do with the setting up of the early
youth movements as altruism. Their early founders seem to have been
at least as much concerned to prevent themselves from being harmed
as they were to do good to others.[14] As Dr Scott Lidgett put it, in
advocating the Wesley Guild for the Methodist Church, 'the sooner we
recognize that recreation unorganized is a danger, the better.'[15]
Before 1914, youth movements were a part of what the sociologist
might term the culturally organized processes of formal and informal
social control mechanisms tending to reduce or prevent potential
adolescent deviance.[16] The deterrent effect of youth movements,
for example, was often publicized in an effort to extract further
subscriptions from the middle-class:

> It would be well if people would realize how much their safety,
> their comfort and their peace depend upon the work of the

Brigades in this country. Were it not for the self-sacrificing efforts of the men who labour amongst our lads in the slums of London and other large cities, it might well be that those who are now asked to give their little guineas to the work might be called upon to pay substantially for a largely augmented police force.[17]

William Smith, the founder of the Boys' Brigade, was among the first to realize that the successful propagation of a 'manly' religion to the young required it to be articulated in cultural and organizational forms more in keeping with an age of nationalism and militarism:

> I knew that every lad was proud of being a British boy, and yet they seemed rather ashamed of being Christian boys [he told an American audience]. This convinced me that the Sunday School would become more popular with the lads if we had an organization that appealed to their national pride. The first company was organized, and the quick response convinced me that I had reasoned correctly.[18]

How far youth movements helped to nurture nationalism and how far they were an effect of its preponderance in British society at this time cannot really be answered with any precision. Yet it is noticeable that Smith was given to making fashionable social Darwinist remarks to his Bible Class, such as : 'no nation ever yet attained true greatness or influence without going through the training and discipline of war.'[19] Militarism was a lot less unpopular in the late-nineteenth century than in a later age of conscription, for 'in those days everybody encouraged the military spirit.'[20] Romantic Victorian attitudes to the glamour of war, reflected in G. A. Henty's boys' fiction,[21] gave their Wolseleys and Gordons more social prestige than generals were to enjoy in the aftermath of the Boer War or the First World War. The Victorian cult of the Christian Soldier as Hero did a great deal to make the military structure of the Boys' Brigade socially acceptable.[22]

Referring to the Boys' Brigade as 'A Juvenile Citizen Army', one local newspaper did not doubt that the Volunteer Force would be richly the gainer by the new youth movement. 'It is in this sense, no doubt correct,' opined this newspaper in 1889, 'that society was not a generation or so ago so well constituted for the engrafting of a religious shoot upon the military trunk.'[23] Thus the military values of the Volunteers secured a greater degree of Church and Nonconformist recognition through the agency of the Boys' Brigade than they might

otherwise have found.[24] 'There can be no doubt that one individual
result of the work of the Brigades', declared Smith himself in 1910,
'has been to popularize the idea of military service among the people
generally.'[25] It is against this general background of tolerance for
military values, in the guise of middle-class respectability, that imitations of the original Scottish prototype began to make their appearance
in London during the 1890s:

> It must strike the observer of events that in one way or another
> society is running pretty freely to militarism, [commented one
> editorial] we are brought more and more into the presence of the
> military spirit.[26]

Even Herbert Spencer, the arch social Darwinist, repudiated as inimical
to the English liberal tradition which he upheld, the methods of militarism closely allied to the imperialism which he felt had penetrated
social life.[27]

Although nationalism and militarism may have been the basic historical moulds within which youth movements were formed, there was
also a deep general undercurrent of imperialism running through many
of the more florid statements of their leadership. Yet by the 1900s,
the glamorous and aggressive style of imperialism found in earlier
decades had become subordinated to the strengthening of the Empire's
existing frontiers. 'These are no days of aggrandisement; nor is there
need,' wrote one Colonel in 1909, 'but these are surely days for realizing
Empire.'[28] Preservation rather than expansion invariably led to a
concomitant concern for imperial defence to face the German threat.
Thus Baden-Powell felt obliged to devote a sub-section in the first
edition of the famous handbook, *Scouting for Boys*, to 'How the
Empire must be held'.[29] In this context, youth movements ensured
the continuity of certain broadly conservative, conformist attitudes,
particularly towards the British Empire, that were actively resisting
change in British society. Some among them clearly saw their role as
that of training the rising generation to take up the reins of Empire
from their faltering predecessors:

> The working-class boy is, without doubt, just the boy to whom we
> must look for the Briton of the future. What is implanted in the
> boy of today will develop in the man who will make or mar the
> National Empire of tomorrow [claimed an exponent of compulsory

cadet training as] the proper solution for the national defence of the Empire.[30]

It was not until the 1920s that youth movements following a positive anti-imperialist and anti-militarist approach emerged to offer an alternative ideological foundation to that of the more main-stream organizations. An account of the origins and ideas of these small woodcraft groups has thus been included in order to offer a contrast to the well-established, much larger and less experimental youth movements.

In what follows, an attempt will be made — however imperfect — to locate the major British youth movements within their common historical situation, an element usually lacking in most of the authorized accounts of their development. To understand why each youth movement should have appeared precisely when and where it did, I have chosen to look at the particular social and cultural circumstances of the late-nineteenth and early-twentieth centuries in which each was rooted. Several of these organizations, particularly the various denominational imitations of the Boys' Brigade, have — until now — been almost entirely overlooked by the historian. If, initially, youth movements appear to emerge only through the tireless activities of certain prominent individuals, it is as products of their historical environment, shaped by contemporary ideological forces, that I have tried to present them — rather than as picturesque aberrations from the social and historical norm. Perhaps, should the past history of British youth movements — the origins of most of those in existence now — be examined with a more open mind as a result of this introductory survey, it may prove relevant to the situation of those adults who carry on work with young people today.

Notes

1. See Paul Wilkinson, 'A Study of English Uniformed Youth Movements, 1883-1935: their origins, development, and social and political influence.' M.A. thesis, University of Wales, 1968, pp. 3-5.
2. See Mass Observation Ltd., sample of 2,000 adults, for the Baden-Powell Scout Guild, Press Release, 'Were you ever a Boy Scout?' 14 April 1967.
3. Viz., the attitude of twentieth-century governments to the Army Cadet Force — they withdrew the War Office cadet grant from 1923 to 1925 and official recognition from 1930 to 1931 — suggests anti-militarist pressures as well as the opportunity to make economies in government spending.
4. See John Gillis, *Youth and History: tradition and change in European age relations, 1760 to the present* (London, 1974), chap. 4.
5. See Louis Heren, *Growing Up Poor in London* (London, 1973, chap. 5,

for his 'weekend escape' from 'the narrow horizon of the tenements and dock walls of Shadwell' in the 2nd City of London Sea Scout Troop.

6.   See John Saville, 'Trade Unions and Free Labour: the background to the Taff Vale Decision' in A. Briggs and J. Saville (eds.), *Essays in Labour History* (London 1960, pp. 317-350; Gareth Stedman-Jones, *Outcast London* (Oxford, 1971), pp. 292-296; David Rubenstein, 'The Sack of the West End, 1886', in David Rubenstein (ed.), *People for the People* (London, 1973), pp. 139-145; E. H. Phelps-Brown, *The Growth of British Industrial Relations* (London, 1959), pp. 89-113.

7.   See Graham Murdock and Robin McCron, 'Consciousness of Generation', *Cultural Studies,* Nos. 7/8, Summer 1975, esp. pp. 192-193; Gillis, *Youth and History*, pp. 141-144.

8.   See Stephen Yeo, 'Capitalism, Leisure and Voluntary Organizations: a preliminary framework for research', duplicated paper delivered on 29 November 1975, at a meeting of the Society for the Study of Labour History on 'The Working Class and Leisure' held at the University of Sussex.

9.   See John Gillis, 'The Evolution of Juvenile Delinquency in England, 1890-1914', *Past and Present,* No. 67 (May, 1975), pp. 96-126.

10.   Col. Bennett, Ms. version of article, 'The Origins of the Army Cadet Force', in 'G' Company Archives, 'Queen's' Cadet Battalion, Stoke Newington, London. This piece appeared in *The Cadet Journal* (November, 1942), p. 151, but without the cited remark.

11.   Baden-Powell, *Scouting for Boys* (London, 1909 edn.), p. 282.

12.   See John Gillis, 'Conformity and Rebellion: contrasting styles of English and German youth, 1900-1933', *History of Education Quarterly,* Vol. XIII, No. 3 (Fall, 1973), p. 253.

13.   Revd M. R. Allnutt, 'The Church Lads' Brigade. What Is It Doing?', leaflet (n.d.), p. 4. Archives of Church Lads' Brigade, London.

14.   See Bernard Davies and Alan Gibson, *The Social Education of the Adolescent* (London, 1967), p. 32.

15.   Cited in Fred Milson, *Youth Work in the 1970 s* (London, 1970), p. 41.

16.   See Howard Becker, *Outsiders: studies in the sociology of deviance* (London, 1963), p. 9; Kai T. Erikson, 'Notes on the Sociology of Deviance' in Howard Becker (ed.), *The Other Side* (London, 1964), pp. 9-21; David Matza, *Becoming Deviant* (London, 1969), pp. 11-12; Edwin M. Lemert, *Human Deviance, Social Problems and Social Control* (New Jersey, 1967), pp. 18-26; Albert K. Cohen, *Deviance and Control* (New Jersey, 1966), *passim.*

17.   *The Catholic Boys' Brigade Gazette*, Vol. 1, No. 2 (July, 1910), p. 5.

18.   Speech by Smith, 23 May 1907, cited in *The American Brigadier*, Vol. 1, No. 10 (July 1967), p. 21.

19.   William Smith, holograph notes, Bible Class exegesis on 'Joshua' (n.d.), p. 7. Archives of 1st Glasgow Co., Boys' Brigade, Scotland.

20.   W. G. Cooper to A. W. Fisher, 12 May 1935; a reference to 1889 and the Southwark Cadet Corps. Letter held in the Cadet Training Centre, Frimley Park, Camberley, Surrey. The term 'militarism' is used here in its perjorative sense of the undue prevalence of the military spirit or its ideals, rather than in its alternative dictionary meaning as the tendencies of the professional soldier.

21.   See John Gooch, 'Attitudes to War in late Victorian and Edwardian England', in Brian Bond and Ian Toy (eds.), *War and Society*, a yearbook of military history (London, 1975), p. 88; J. O. Springhall, The Rise and Fall of Henty's Empire', *Times Literary Supplement*, 3 October 1968; William

Allan, 'G. A. Henty', *The Cornhill Magazine*, Vol. 181. No. 1082, 1974, pp. 71 100.

22. See Olive Anderson, 'The Growth of Christian Militarism in Mid-Victorian Britain', *The English Historical Review*, Vol. LXXXVI (January, 1971), pp. 46-72; typical of the Christian Soldier Hero were Sir Henry Havelock, an Evangelical Baptist general who died during the Indian Mutiny, and General Gordon.

23. The *Thames Valley Times*, 10 April 1889.

24. See Prof. H. J. Hanham, 'Religion and Nationality in the Mid-Victorian Army', M. R. D. Foot (ed.), *War and Society* (London, 1973), pp. 172-174.

25. William Smith to Roger Peacock, 6 June 1910. Cadet Correspondence File, 1910-1911, Boys' Brigade Archives, Fulham, London.

26. The *Thames Valley Times*, op. cit.

27. Herbert Spencer, 'Imperialism and Slavery', in *Facts and Comments*, (London 1902), pp. 112-113.

28. Colonel Coleman, 'Thoughts on Empire Day', *The Patriot*, Vol. II (June, 1909), p. 2. This was the journal of the Essex branch of the National Service League.

29. Baden Powell, op. cit., pp. 267 268.

30. W. Cecil Price, *The Cadet Movement* (n.d. 1917?), proofs, p. 1019, Boys' Brigade Archives, London. This appears to be a contribution to a collection of essays on military issues written during the First World War.

1 'SURE AND STEDFAST'

If Saint Paul was the prophet of manly Christianity and Dr Thomas Arnold its most famous public-school practitioner, then William Alexander Smith, the founder and first Secretary of the Boys' Brigade, must be credited with putting the idea into uniform, drilling it and providing it with a uniquely Scottish dissenting flavour.[1] Smith explained:

> By associating Christianity with all that was most noble and manly in a boy's sight, we would be going a long way to disabuse his mind of the idea that there is anything effeminate or weak about Christianity.[2]

No milk-and-water religion here. But why should the Boys' Brigade have originated in Glasgow rather than in any other late-Victorian city? An explanation requires some consideration of the peculiarly Scottish historical ingredients shaping the emergence of the first mass, voluntary youth movement in Britain — and the career of William Smith (as a businessman, Volunteers officer and Sunday School teacher) offers a useful summation of the most important of them.

William Smith's life spanned the outbreak of the Crimean War to that of the First World War.[3] He was born in 1854 near Thurso, about 20 miles west of John O'Groats, into a family with strong military traditions.[4] Information about his early life remains as elusive as the character of the man himself, but it is known that early in 1868 his father died while on business in China.[5] Subsequently young William, the eldest son, was packed off to work for his uncle in Glasgow — a wholesale dealer in 'soft' goods, largely shawls, to the South American market.[6] In 1874, under the influence of Moody and Sankey's Evangelical crusade in Scotland,[7] Smith took the step of abandoning the Church of Scotland, in which he had been brought up, to join the College Free Church, of which his uncle was already an Elder, in West Glasgow's prosperous Hillhead.[8] Here he came under the powerful spell of the darkly handsome Revd George Reith, father of the first Director-General of the BBC and an enthusiastic follower of Moody and Sankey.[9] In the same year, coincidentally, Smith joined the crack Glasgow Volunteer Regiment, the 1st Lanarkshire Rifles, thereby further alienating his uncle, who already objected to young Smith's over-ambitious business methods.[10]

William Smith's personality and motivation must remain something of an enigma, for he has left little behind in the way of autobiographical information. One biographer had to suggest the exercise of the imagination to fill in the details of his life, while another stresses how dull it was — as Smith never seemed to do anything really exciting from the day he was born until the day he died.[11] There is, however, no necessity to subscribe to either view for, although some hagiographical sources present him as a living incarnation of Christian manliness, Smith's private correspondence demonstrates that he could display all the qualities of a typically thrifty and canny Scot.[12] Naturally modest, unselfish and self-effacing, he was at the same time hard-working, masterful, somewhat austere and rather a martinet.[13] Twice married, his two sons by his first marriage both followed him into the movement, Stanley Smith acting as Brigade Secretary from 1925 until 1954.

The cultural superstructure provided by Bible Classes and branches of the YMCA which helped to make the Boys' Brigade possible, owed a great deal to the stimulation of youth work in Glasgow as a result of Moody and Sankey's revival of middle-class Scottish Evangelical Christianity.[14] Indirectly, the building of the North Woodside Mission, the birthplace of the Boys' Brigade, owed much to the inspiration of Dwight Moody's preaching — even if the actual idea of building mission churches in working-class areas of Glasgow had originally been proposed by Reith's predecessor at the College Free Church.[15] William Smith, as one of the Free Church's young Sunday School teachers, was drafted in to help with the newly created Mission congregation; this consisted largely of the 'respectable' artisan working class in a district rapidly being 'built up' with tenements.[16]

Starting as Secretary of the Sunday School Teachers' Society, by 1880 Smith had set up a Young Men's Club, closely modelled on the YMCA, to add to the Mission's numerous other social activities.[17] Then, after a dispute over both his business and military plans, Smith precipitately left his uncle's service to go into the importing trade himself, in partnership with his brother Donald, as a wholesale 'shawl dealer' or 'manufacturer' in West Nile Street, Glasgow.[18] Already both the chief facets of Smith's career and the social milieu from which the Boys' Brigade was to recruit its first officers can be distinguished in embryo: the Volunteers, the Hillhead district of Glasgow, the Scottish Free Church and the Sunday School. It awaited only a spark to fuse them all together in the shape of the formation in 1883 of the Boys' Brigade.

Great acts of creative synthesis are seldom performed in a vacuum. While a tendency towards a greater emphasis being placed on nationalism and militarism in British society as a whole in the 1880s may have provided the tinder which helped kindle the fire, the inflammable material was provided in Glasgow itself by the 1st Lanarkshire Rifle Volunteers. And the 'spark' that set these elements alight was William Smith's search for a method of controlling the rowdy working-class boys attending his Mission Sunday School. But whoever actually suggested to Smith that he adopt the military organization and discipline of the Volunteers to improve Sunday School discipline and maintain order,[19] it is extremely unlikely that without his own part-time military training the Boys' Brigade would ever have been created:

> To the Volunteer movement we are indebted for this novel and interesting organization [wrote a Glaswegian in 1887] which seeks to use military drill and discipline for the religious and moral improvement of the boys in our mission districts and Sabbath schools.[20]

More precisely, as one of the original members of Smith's first Glasgow company put it, the Brigade came to serve a particular function for a more specific age group:

> When we reached thirteen most of us felt we were too big for the Sunday School, and there was a gap of a few years until we were able to join the YMCA at seventeen. To fill this gap, Captain Smith formed the Boys' Brigade. During that gap period, many working-class boys ran wild, became hooligans and street-corner loafers. What else was there for them in those days, to do?[21]

Smith also reasoned that a new uniformed organization appealing to a boy's sense of patriotism and martial spirit would serve as a useful instrument for a primarily religious end.

On 4 October 1883, after obtaining the somewhat reluctant permission of Reith and the Kirk Session, the Boys' Brigade (as the 1st Glasgow Company was then known) was launched fully-fledged with its own crest, title, motto and object,[22] in the Mission Hall, North Woodside Road, where it was to drill for the next 90 years. One of the original recruits, James Thomson, recollects that 'hundreds wanted to join . . . but a good many were rejected because they wouldn't

attend Sabbath School.'[23] While with regard to discipline, a boy
arriving one minute late was not allowed to fall-in on drill parade, and
no one was permitted two consecutive absences without good reason.
With Smith receiving the energetic assistance of the two Hill brothers,[24]
those boys who remained in the 1st Glasgow Company, despite the
strict conditions for continued membership, were to become a potential source for expansion. In the course of this first session, dummy
rifles, a Club Room, and the familiar uniform of 'pill-box' cap, belt
and haversack — which were to provide the model for every company
that followed — were all rapidly introduced.[25] And in December
1884, the first BB Bible Class was held, thus allowing Smith to draw
on a wider range of recruits than attended his Sunday School classes
and to assert a semi-autonomous status within the Church.

The social composition of the original company formed in Glasgow
tended to reflect the nature of its initial Sunday School recruitment.
It was drawn from the sons of a Mission Church congregation in a predominantly 'respectable' working-class area of West Glasgow — hardly
the 'unwashed slum boys' that some accounts suggest. A sample of
membership in the 1890s, taken from early enrolment books, demonstrates that sons of skilled manual workers or those with fathers in
'white collar' occupations, clearly prevail over a negligible number
with unskilled or semi-skilled parents.

Table 1: 1st Glasgow Enrolment Figures, 1890-1895[26]
(Parental Occupation)

	1890-1891	1891-1892	1892-1893	1893-1894	1894-1895	Total	%
Skilled manual*	17	2	5	6	6	36	72
Lower-middle+	4	2	6	2	-	14	27
Unskilled†	2	-	-	1	-	3	1
Total	23	4	11	9	6	53	100

* = joiners, cabinet-makers, engine-fitters, shoe-makers, masons, etc.
+ = salesmen, clerks, travellers, insurance agents, drapers, grocers, etc.
† = labourers, commissionaires.

The arrival of the Boys' Brigade on the streets of Glasgow coincided
with a slight lull in the city's impressive nineteenth-century economic

progress, her ship-building boom intermittently threatened by international competition; although the versatility of Glasgow's industrial
complex tended to reduce class tensions, at least until the 1900s.[27]
Nonetheless, the repercussions of economic uncertainty felt among
Glasgow's mercantile business community were exacerbated by the
various tensions associated with the fast accelerating urbanization and
consequent over-crowding of areas like North Woodside, made more
conspicuous by being adjacent to the middle-class residential housing
in North West Glasgow.[28] So although the city could afford to be
proud of a long continuing tradition of philanthropic youth work,[29]
under the influence of Moody and Sankey's omnipresent Evangelical
revival, wealthy industrialists embarked on conscience-salving expenditure on the Boys' Brigade as much as from a pervasive sense of social
anxiety as from any other cause.[30] Discipline, punctuality and a
strict obedience to orders from his men were, after all, as desirable to
the Clydeside dock employer or manufacturer as to the Boys' Brigade
drill sergeant.

On 26 January 1885, after a meeting at Smith's terraced house in
fashionable Hillhead to form the basis for a national movement — since
there were by then five other companies in the process of formation in
Glasgow — a Brigade Council and Constitution were formally adopted.[31]
Receiving the powerful patronage of successive Presidents, among them
Lord Guthrie and the Earl of Aberdeen, the number of Boys' Brigade
companies grew all over Scotland. Glasgow, though, retained its overall
numerical lead: of the 40 Scottish companies in existence by 1886,
25 were in Glasgow. Despite its being Scottish led and inspired, during
the 1890s there was a considerable expansion of the Boys' Brigade
over the border until, in terms of boy strength, Scotland was ultimately
overtaken by England and Wales (Table 2). Yet, even in 1891, almost
half of all the British companies registered were Scottish Presbyterian in
religious composition (Table 3). The average Boys' Brigade Lieutenant
at this time was likely to be a young Sunday School teacher in his early
twenties, who had previously served in a company elsewhere.[32]

Once the initial pattern of activities had been imposed, the Boys'
Brigade soon settled down to a steady if unspectacular growth under
Smith's stern paternal leadership. As full-time Secretary from 1888, he
supervized a weekly routine of drill, Bible Class and Club Room,
disturbed only by the much-heralded annual camp or the occasional
field-day to raise company funds. While by modern-day standards,
the original programme may appear either crude or unimaginative, it
must have held a far greater appeal to the boy confined to the drab

Table 2: Boys' Brigade U.K. Membership, 1884-1889[33]

Year	England & Wales		Scotland		Ireland		Totals	
	Cos.	Boys	Cos.	Boys	Cos.	Boys	Cos.	Boys
1884			1	30			1	30
1885			5	268			5	268
1886	4	191	40	1,808			44	1,999
1887	10	452	114	5,664			124	6,116
1888	37	1,516	183	8,872			220	10,388
1889	85	3,714	232	10,614	1	44	318	14,372
1890	122	5,023	260	11,109	12	620	394	16,752
1891	143	5,139	252	11,138	23	982	418	17,259
1892	212	9,248	245	10,293	33	1,461	490	21,002
1893	313	13,841	221	9,661	60	2,531	594	26,033
1894	371	16,718	239	10,552	64	2,579	674	29,849
1895	416	17,647	255	11,679	71	3,053	742	32,379
1896	435	18,711	264	11,522	64	2,629	763	32,862
1897	453	18,472	258	12,290	60	2,361	771	33,123
1898	468	18,823	259	12,858	59	2,528	786	34,209
1899	470	19,715	276	12,796	66	2,637	812	35,148

monotony of urban existence in the late-nineteenth century. It would be superfluous to describe company activities at the local level in any great detail, notwithstanding the wide range of available source material,[34] but here is one description that conveys a vivid impression of a typical evening's drill as seen by a sympathetic outsider:

> I watched this carefully for I had gathered that it was the ground work of the Brigade system. Very thorough work it was; for half an hour these boys marched and turned and wheeled, formed fours and column, tied themselves into all sorts of knots and straightened themselves out again, finishing up at the 'double', whereat the floor quaked and a thin stream of mist arose therefrom. Finally they are formed in line, which must be 'dressed' with mathematical precision before 'stand at ease' is ordered.[35]

It is worth pointing out that concert performances, company inspect-

Table 3: Religious Composition of Boys' Brigade Companies,
February 1891.[36]

Religion (Cos.)	Scotland		England		Northern Ireland		Totals	
	No.	%	No.	%	No.	%	No.	%
Presbyterian	201	76	27	19	5	23	233	54
Episcopalian	17	6	60	41	15	68	92	21
Wesleyan/Methodist	1	0.3	27	19	-	-	28	7
Congregational	6	2	12	8	1	4.5	19	4
Baptist	1	0.3	7	5	1	4.5	9	2
Others	40	15	12	8	-	-	52	12
Total	266	100	145	100	22	100	433	100

ions and presentations were among those items of company activities
most prominently reported — as the following table demonstrates:

Table 4: Analysis of Company Reports[37]

	1889-1890	1903-1904
Speeches/addresses	17	-
Concerts	12	20
Company Inspections	27	21
Presentations	17	18
Bands	-	24
Total for these events	73	83
Total events reported	225	270

There followed for the Brigade over 20 years of uninterrupted
expansion throughout the British Isles. Then, in the late 1900s, the
seemingly calm and unruffled surface of the movement's progress was
disturbed by a succession of traumatic events that were to determine
its future development in the years to come. The first of these, from

1907 to 1908, was the setting up of the Boy Scouts by Baden-Powell, which owed not a little to the encouragement he had received in the past from William Smith.[38] Numbers in Scouting rapidly outstripped those of any other youth movement even before the First World War. Next, from 1909 to 1911, came a miscalculated attempt by R. B. Haldane, the Liberal Secretary of State for War, to incorporate the Boys' Brigade into a national cadet force to be administered by the Territorials. Finally, and probably the most disturbing event of all within the Brigade itself, came William Smith's premature death from over-work at the age of sixty — only a few months before the outbreak of war in 1914.

To refer only to the second of these testing events in the Brigade's history, it is a tribute to Smith's clear-sighted and skilful management of the Boys' Brigade that, before his death, he was able to steer it away from the seductive shoals of co-operation with the War Office and Haldane's famous 'second line' of national defence. Briefly, Haldane's general plan was to absorb all the uniformed youth movements into one homogeneous whole in order to give them a *locus standi* as recognized cadet units affiliated to and acting as feeders for their local Territorial Force Association.[39] The Army Council's Cadet Regulations issued in 1910 in effect presented an ultimatum to the various brigades. They were told to apply to their local Territorials for official 'recognition' as cadets or forfeit the military and financial assistance which they had been accustomed to receive from the War Office.[40] William Smith had no intention of forsaking the religious aims of his movement in order to forge inopportune links with the military machine, despite the constant accusations of militarism or jingoism that had been levelled at the 'Brigade idea' by pacifists and some Nonconformists in the 1880s and 1890s.[41]

> It is becoming increasingly clear [Smith wrote to the leader of the more pliable Church Lads' Brigade] that the Boys' Brigade would make a serious mistake, from the point of view of its true purpose, if it accepted official recognition by the Army Council.[42]

Notwithstanding the strong pressures brought to bear by the War Office,[43] as Roger Peacock, at that time London Secretary of the Brigade, remembers, 'Smith was adamant in his refusal to make any compact between the BB and the military authorities.'[44] His intransigence was rooted in his belief that Haldane intended to compel the brigades to become an integral part of the country's armed forces and

that this would result in irreparable damage to the reputation of the
Boys' Brigade as a primarily religious organization.[45] Thus armed with
a conviction of the essential rightness of his campaign, Smith was not
averse to resisting War Office tactics by employing some worldly
political intrigue of his own:

> Our idea is that Mr Haldane might be quite alive to the fact that
> they stand to lose in the country just now, [he wrote of the Lib-
> erals at the time of the 1910 General Election] if there is any
> sense of irritation against the government, as represented by the
> War Office, [and] they might be anxious, from political motives,
> to remove any cause of friction.[46]

Of more importance in the struggle to resist any official connection
with the military was the underestimation by the War Office of the
strength of public support in Scotland for the stand taken by the Boys'
Brigade, while by an overwhelming vote the rank-and-file of the movement also rejected official recognition as cadets.[47] Yet subsequently,
as a war-time measure in 1917 in order to protect the Boys' Brigade
from the competition of military cadet battalions then in process of
formation, a decision was made to allow individual companies to apply
for cadet recognition by the Territorials.[48] Ultimately, in 1924, all
official military links with the State were severed when the Brigade
Executive decided not to allow companies to continue as recognized
units under the new, more restrictive, Army Council regulations, which
required affiliation to an army unit and a syllabus laid down by the
military.[49]

The Boys' Brigade's chief English rival, the Church Lads' Brigade —
which had accepted full recognition as cadets in 1911 — was to experience a steady decline in numbers over the inter-war period, largely
owing to the emergence of a public mood of anti-militarism in the 1920s.
By contrast, the Boys' Brigade, after an initial drop in numbers in 1919,
showed a steady expansion from 1921 onwards, until by 1937 they had
well over twice the number of companies active in England and Wales
as their Church of England counterpart. As Table 5 indicates, the Boys'
Brigade continued to expand their companies throughout the 1930s,
although even as late as 1939 almost 44 per cent of their boy strength
was still concentrated in Scotland and Northern Ireland. Despite this
increase, the Boys' Brigade came nowhere near approaching the membership of the considerably more powerful Scout movement, whose growth
had always been more conspicuous and dramatic.[50]

Table 5: Boys' Brigade U.K. Membership, 1930-1940[51]

Year	England & Wales		Scotland		Ireland		Totals	
	Cos.	Boys	Cos.	Boys	Cos.	Boys	Cos.	Boys
1930	1,434	46,366	700	28,811	123	4,162	2,257	79,339
1931	1,485	46,734	716	28,476	125	4,154	2,326	79,364
1932	1,518	49,558	736	30,405	141	5,070	2,395	85,033
1933	1,590	53,630	771	33,447	149	5,727	2,510	92,804
1934	1,662	54,854	809	35,922	157	5,986	2,628	96,762
1935	1,674	51,235	839	35,572	160	5,702	2,673	92,509
1936	1,678	50,327	872	35,201	167	5,951	2,717	91,479
1937	1,689	50,371	875	34,728	170	5,968	2,734	91,067
1938	1,694	50,941	889	35,061	173	6,136	2,756	92,138
1939	1,745	52,468	896	34,957	180	6,230	2,821	93,655
1940	1,558	44,530	779	26,655	161	5,564	2,498	76,749

And in the less authoritarian, more relaxed society of the post-1945 decades in Britain, it was Scouting that was to capture a far wider audience than the uniformed, military-structured, single-sex, religious youth movements. The Boy Scouts had always been more flexible, more designed to accommodate themselves to changing cultural and social patterns than the 'brigades', whose appeal to boys declined in the more 'affluent' circumstances of the 1950s and 1960s.[52] Increased purchasing power among the young, enlarged commercial leisure provision, more extra-curricular activities in schools and major shifts in teenage interests, have all reduced the unique appeal of the Boys' Brigade which was so apparent 90 years ago. In general, the weakening of traditional authority, with changes in moral standards and the loosening ties of family and community, as well as widening opportunities in education, work and leisure, make it unrealistic of the Boys' Brigade to expect any dramatic reversal of existing trends in membership.[53]

Notes

1.   See Norman Vance, 'The Ideal of Manliness' in *Times Educational Supplement*, 28 September 1973, p. 24; E. C. Mack and W. H. G. Armytage, *Thomas Hughes* (London 1952), pp. 97-98.

2.   William A. Smith, 'The Boys' Brigade', leaflet based on a paper read at the Scottish National Sabbath School Convention at Arbroath, 30 September 1887, p. 2. Reprinted from *The Sabbath School Magazine*, December 1887. Cf. C. H. Spurgeon, *A Good Start* (London, 1898), pp. 16-17; W. A. Smith, *The Story of the Boys' Brigade* (Glasgow, 1888), pp. 8-9.

3.   William Smith (1854-1914). See Biographical Notes.

4.   His father, Major David Smith, of the local Caithness Volunteer Artillery Corps, had served as an ensign of the 7th Dragoon Guards during the South African 'Kaffir War' of 1849-1850, while his grandfather had been Adjutant in the 78th Highland Regiment of Foot or 'Ross-shire Buffs' and, according to family legend, had fought at Waterloo.

5.   Major Smith — a member of the intrepid breed of Scottish merchant-adventurers who pioneered trade in the British Empire — had gone to China in connection with the Labuan Coal Company, of which he was a director, only to die of cholera in Swatow when his eldest son, William, was thirteen.

6.   See Autobiographical notes, 1868-1872, loose holograph Mss., Boys' Brigade Archives, Fulham, London.

7.   Whether or not he was actually converted by the two American Evangelists must remain an open question. See F. P. Gibbon, *William A. Smith of the Boys' Brigade* (London, 1934), pp. 30-31.

8.   There is extant a diary for 1875 kept by Smith, with the crucial events of 1874 marked in red ink to underline their significance, viz., 12 February 1874: 'heard Moody and Sankey for the first time'; 12 April 1874: 'I joined the Church'. In 1885 Smith was ordained a Deacon of this Church. Diary consulted at Boys' Brigade Headquarters in January 1972.

9.   See Revd W. M. Clow, *Dr. George Smith: a Scottish ministry* (London, 1928), p. 101. Reith became Chaplain of the 1st Glasgow Company of the Boys' Brigade from 1883 until his death in 1919. The College Free Church burnt down in 1903.

10.   See F. P. Gibbon, p. 26. By 1881 Smith had become a Lieutenant in the Volunteers; he retired as a Lieutenant-Colonel in 1908. Eventually, the 1st Lanarkshire Rifle Volunteers became the 5/8th Battalion, the Cameronians (Scottish Rifles).

11.   Roger S. Peacock, *Pioneer of Boyhood: story of Sir William A. Smith* (Glasgow, 1954), p. 16; Ronald Selby Wright, *Great Men* (London, 1951), p. 21.

12.   Once he refused to pay a rail fare, claiming to the General Manager of the Glasgow District Subway Company that he had lost his ticket. On another occasion, he left a house he was renting after living in it for ten years because, he argued, the estate agents refused to meet his conditions with regard to re-decoration. See Smith Correspondence, 18 June 1900; 2-4 February 1899, Letter Book, Vol. III, 1899-1900. Boys' Brigade Archives, Fulham, London.

13.   See G. Stanley Smith, 'My Father' in *The Boys' Brigade Jubilee Bulletin*, 4 September 1933, p. 3; Alexander Martin, 'Memories of the 1st Glasgow', 13 November 1956, typescript, p. 4 (kindly loaned by the author); the Memorial Number of *The Boys' Brigade Gazette*, Vol. XXII, No. 10, 1 June 1914.

14.   See George Adam Smith, *The Life of Henry Drummond* (London, 1899), pp. 57-61; Kathleen Heasman, *Evangelicals in Action* (London, 1962), p. 125; J. C. Pollock, *Moody without Sankey* (London, 1963), chap. 15; Clyde Binfield, *George Williams and the Y.M.C.A.* (London, 1973), pp.

212-215.

15. Cf. Revd Robert Buchanan, *The City's Spiritual Wants and the Christian Church's Duty* (Glasgow, 1871). An address delivered on 28 November 1871 in City Hall, Glasgow, to a Free Church meeting. Until his death in 1875, Buchanan was the Senior Minister at College Free Church, leader of the Free Church in Glasgow, and a restraining hand upon the Evangelical enthusiasm of Reith.

16. Originally in South Woodside – where it had become necessary to vacate the premises owing to a compulsory purchase – the Mission followed the migration of dwelling-house tenants to North Woodside, not far from the middle-class, residential Hillhead where Smith lived. See William Ewing (ed.), *Annals of the Free Church of Scotland*, Vol. II (Edinburgh, 1914), p. 96; Clow, *Reith*, p. 135; Henry Brougham Morton (ed.), *A Hillhead Album* (Glasgow, 1973).

17. Viz., Bands of Hope, Ladies' Visiting and Clothing Society, Tract Distribution, Childrens' Church, Mothers' Meetings, Student Missionaries and a Young Women's Meeting. See Anon., *Free College Church Annual Reports,* 1877-1888, Scottish Record Office, Edinburgh, Scotland.

18. Glasgow business records verify the existence of Smith, Smith and Company from 1879 until 1881 when, owing to his brother's business incapacity hampering the new venture, a partnership was offered to Smith's friend, James Findlay. Although Smith left active business management in 1888 – Findlay having already moved on to become manager of the Irrawaddy Flotilla Company in Burma – the company name, Smith, Findlay and Co., survived until the Great Crash of 1929. See Register of Companies, Scottish Business Archives, Edinburgh, Scotland.

19. One version credits Smith's business partner, James Findlay, with the original inspiration: Gibbon, p. 32; another suggests the Revd George Reith: Peter Stewart, 'A Message about the Founder of the Boys' Brigade', Aberdeen Battalion, message No. 4, Broadcasting, 23 October 1924, p. 2. Document kindly loaned by A. S. Martin, Kilmacolm, Renfrewshire. Scotland.

20. David Howie, *A History of the 1st. Lanarkshire Rifle Volunteers* (Glasgow, 1887), p. 399, Mitchell Library, Glasgow Room. 'All the Companies are drilled by gentlemen who take an interest in the religious side of the work', wrote Smith, 'who are nearly all members of the Volunteer Service'. Letter of 13 July 1885, Letter Book, Vol. 1, 1885, Boys' Brigade Archives, Fulham, London.

21. William Wylie cited in Rushworth Fogg, 'A Scotsman Started It All' in *The Scotsman* (1954) p. 24; cf. 'The Two Surviving Members Talk to Stedfast Magazine' in *Stedfast Magazine*, No. 4, (January, 1954), p. 3.

22. The crest of the Brigade was an anchor, its motto 'Sure and Stedfast' (Epistle to the Hebrews, chap. vi: verse 19), and its object: 'the advancement of Christ's Kingdom among Boys, and the promotion of habits of Reverence, Discipline, Self-Respect, and all that tends towards a true Christian Manliness.' It was not until 1893 that 'Obedience' was inserted as the first of the habits to be promoted. See Austin E. Birch, *The Story of the Boys' Brigade* (London, 1959), p. 22. 'Stedfast' is the biblical spelling.

23. Cited in Rushworth Fogg, p. 25.

24. The Hill brothers, James and John, were the first officers of the first company and close confidants of Smith: they shared with him membership of the Volunteers, the YMCA and Sunday School teaching at the Mission Hall – ideal as qualifications for Boys' Brigade officers. After leaving Glasgow they both became Anglican clergymen: John became Vicar of

Borbury, near Wakefield, and James was made Vicar of Lightcliffe, Yorkshire. See Gibbon, p. 38, fn. 1.

25. The uniform, to be worn over a boy's ordinary working clothes, cost in
all less than two shillings. The guns used for drill purposes, and the cause
of much critical comment, were models with iron barrels, leather slings,
regular spring actions but no connection between barrel and trigger,
costing about four shillings each.

26. Sources: 1st Glasgow Company Enrolment Books, North Woodside Hall,
Glasgow; Glasgow Electoral Registers, Mitchell Library, Glasgow Room.
Only the initial appearance of a name enrolled has been considered;
earlier enrolment books either no longer exist or do not offer sufficient
information to be tabulated.

27. See Iain Hutchinson, 'Politics and Society in Mid-Victorian Glasgow, 1846-
1886', University of Edinburgh, D.Phil. thesis, 1974, p. 36.

28. See C. M. Allan, 'The Genesis of British Urban Re-Development with
special reference to Glasgow' in *The Economic History Review*, Vol. XVIII,
No. 3, 2nd ser., 1965, pp. 598-613; W. H. Bull, 'Working Class Housing
in Glasgow, 1886-1902', University of Strathclyde, M.Litt. thesis, 1973,
passim; John Butt, 'Working Class Housing in Glasgow, 1851-1914', in
Stanley D. Chapman (ed.), *The History of Working Class Housing*(Newton
Abbot, 1971), p. 57-92.

29. Viz., the backing of a confederacy of Evangelical businessmen was as
forthcoming for William Quarrier's working boys' brigades (for shoe-
blacks, newsboys and railway station parcel-boys) and Orphan Cottage
Homes of the 1860s and 1870s, as it was for William Smith's Boys'
Brigade of the 1880s. See Alexander Gammie, *William Quarrier and the
Story of the Orphan Homes of Scotland* (London, 1936), p. 99; Revd John
Urquhart, *The Life Story of William Quarrier* (London, 1900); Iain Hutch-
inson thesis, pp. 195-198.

30. In 1888, when Smith left his business to become full-time Secretary of the
Boys' Brigade, the most generous offer to guarantee him a salary came from
large-scale Clydeside manufacturers: either leaders of dissenting radicalism
in Glasgow or members of the wealthy College Free Church congregation,
such as Smith's future second father-in-law, William A. Campbell, the owner
of a large warehouse-firm business. See copy of a subscription document
guaranteeing Smith's salary and countersigned acknowledgement, McGregor
Donald and Co., 1888; document kindly loaned to me by Hugh McCallum,
Bearsden, Glasgow, Scotland.

31. At this meeting, the anchor crest, title and motto of the original company
were adopted, although in September 1885 the constitution was later
redrafted to cope with an even larger movement. For the complete text of
this revised constitution, see Gibbon, pp. 60-62. At the First Annual
Meeting of the Brigade Council, on 12 October 1885, Smith was elected
Secretary and J. Carfrae Alston, head of a firm of bonded tobacco ware-
houses, was made President.

32. Of a sample of 150 Boys' Brigade officers, over half of them Lieutenants,
enrolled between 1894 and 1920, 35 per cent were in their twenties,
51 per cent had a Sunday School or Bible Class background and 26 per
cent had previous Boys' Brigade training or experience. Source: Enrolment
Forms, Particulars of Officers, Boys' Brigade Archives, London.

33. Source: Statistics compiled by Miss M. D. Ellis, Senior Records Assistant,
Boys' Brigade Headquarters, London. From 1900 to 1915 only total U.K.
figures are available.

34. On the activities of the Glasgow companies alone there are the following

anonymous accounts: *A History of the Glasgow Battalion* (Glasgow, 1891); *The 176th Glasgow Company of the Boys' Brigade,* 1887-1937 (Glasgow, 1937); *The 26th Glasgow, 1886-1946* (Glasgow, 1946); 'The 4th Kirkaldy Company', in *The Boys' Brigade Officers' Handbook* (Glasgow, 1930); *After Fifty Years, a history of the 1st Bearsden Co., B.B., 1898-1948* (Glasgow, 1948); 'For Fifty Years: a brief history of the 1st Glasgow Co., B.B.', *The Anchor,* 1933 Jubilee Issue.

35. Anon., 'How the Boys' Brigade came to our School', BB leaflet No. 7., n.d. (1890s), BM.

36. Source: J. C. Alston, 'Origins, Progress and Present Position of the Movement' in *The Boys' Brigade Gazette,* Vol. III, 2 February 1891, p. 166.

37. Sources: *The Boys' Brigade Gazette,* 1889-1890; *The Brigadier,* 1903-1904. The absence of speeches from 1903-1904 company reports can be accounted for by their more routine nature at this date, and of bands from 1889-1890 by either their comparative rarity or insufficient solemnity.

38. See chap. 3, fn. 48.

39. See R. B. Haldane, 'The Future of the Boys' Brigade and the Cadet Movement', address of 10 October 1917, *Proceedings of the Royal Philosophical Society of Glasgow,* Vol. XLIX, 1917/1918 (Glasgow, 1918), pp. 1-9.

40. See *Regulations Governing the Formation and Administration of Cadet Corps:* draft and official copy issued with special Army Order, provisional (London, HMSO, 1910), War Office Library; Hamilton to Haldane, February-March 1910, War Office 32/9 Cadets/227/General Policy, PRO, London.

41. See the interesting debate on 'militarism' at the Sunday School Union Anniversary Meeting held on the Boys' Brigade, reported in a special supplement to The *Sunday School Chronicle,* 11 May 1888, pp. 246-248; on the issue of 'jingoism' in the Boys' Brigade, there is a report of a conference organised by the Liverpool Sunday School Union on 'The Peace Society and the Boys' Brigade' in *The Boys' Brigade Gazette,* Vol. 1, No. 6, 1 March 1890, pp. 95-96.

42. William Smith to Walter Gee, 22 March 1911. Cadet Correspondence File, 1910-1911, Boys' Brigade Archives, Fulham, London.

43. According to Smith, despite War Office protestations to the contrary, Haldane was 'most certainly bringing pressure to bear by every means open to him to compel us to come in, by making it very uncomfortable for us to stay out.' William Smith to Roger Peacock, 17 March 1911, op. cit. For refusing to comply, the following 'privileges' were withdrawn from the Boys' Brigade: eligibility for a government capitation grant, inspection by uniformed military officers, and the right to hire army camping equipment.

44. Roger Peacock, *Pioneer of Boyhood,* p. 108.

45. See William Smith to Brigadier-General G. F. Ellison (War Office), 4 March 1911, Cadet Correspondence file, op. cit. Smith was basically correct in his interpretation of War Office motives, viz. 'We agree strongly with the view you expressed as to the desirability of linking up the various boys' organizations with the Territorial Force.' Lord Lucas to the 12th Earl of Meath, 1 October 1909, Meath Papers, Killruddery, Bray, Co. Wicklow, Ireland.

46. William Smith to R. G. Hayes (Admiralty), 24 November 1910, Cadet Correspondence File, op. cit. The London Secretary of the Boys' Brigade also invited the Territorial Force to use its influence with the Army Council to help secure the Brigade's lost privileges. Cf. Roger S. Peacock to Secretary of London Territorial force Association, 30 December 1910, ibid.

47.	In November 1910, a plebiscite of 1,161 companies in the Boys' Brigade indicated that 87 per cent of all the officers were against official recognition, while 89 per cent of the Churches with which they were connected and 88 per cent of parents and supporters were considered to disapprove as well. See *The Boys' Brigade Gazette,* 1 January 1911, p. 66.

48.	In fact, only 291 out of 6,368 companies in Britain did apply for cadet recognition – and of these only 63 companies actually adopted khaki uniform. But it is probable that, when they ceased to belong in 1924, there were some 15,000 Boys' Brigade cadets in all.

49.	See Boys' Brigade, Cadet Recognition File, 1923-24, op. cit., and Boys' Brigade, *Annual Report,* 1923-24, *passim.*

50.	While the number of Church Lads' Brigade companies in England and Wales fell from 1,460 in 1919 to 794 in 1931 (Wilkinson, p. 55), the Boys' Brigade expanded from 480 companies in 1919 to 1,485 in 1931. Yet the Boy Scout membership figure for England and Wales in 1931 (excluding Sea Scouts and Rover Scouts) was alone a total of 174,168, compared to 46,734 for the Boys' Brigade; and Wolf Cub membership was 137,512 compared to 48,331 Life Boys in the whole U.K.

51.	Source: statistics compiled by Miss M. D. Ellis, Senior Records Assistant, Boys' Brigade Headquarters, London.

52.	From a total membership figure of around 91,000 in 1960, the Boys' Brigade had shrunk to 63,000 by 1970, although there were signs in the 1970s of a revival in certain regions, particularly in Northern Ireland. The Church Lads' Brigade, on the other hand, had a total membership of about 11,000 boys in the late 1960s. By comparison, the Boy Scouts had a total strength of well over half a million in Britain alone.

53.	See The Boys' Brigade, *The Haynes Committee Report,* February 1964, Brigade Headquarters, intro., p. 7; James H. Leicester & W. A. James (eds.), *Trends in the Services for Youth* (London, 1967), Section V.

2 RELIGION IN UNIFORM

The outstanding success of of the Boys' Brigade as a youth movement in time led other Churches to consider imitating Smith's creation — notwithstanding its outwardly inter-denominational character. They set out to achieve a similar blend of recreation and military training with the intention of binding the adolescent closer to his religious or ethnic community. Curiously, most of these adaptations of the original Scottish prototype emerged in the London of the last decade of the nineteenth century: the Church Lads' Brigade in a Fulham Parish Church in 1891, the Jewish Lads' Brigade in a Jewish School in Whitechapel in 1895, and the Catholic Boys' Brigade in a boys' club in Bermondsey in 1896. Among the larger 'brigades' of the 1890s, only the non-military Boys' Life Brigade — started by a Congregationalist Minister in Nottingham in 1899 — was founded outside the metropolis.

The initial inspiration for these 'brigades' was derivative. In some cases, they imitated each other rather than the original Boys' Brigade. Despite this, the pattern of their respective histories is still, almost by definition, unique to each 'brigade'. If today, only the Boys' Brigade maintains any real currency in the popular imagination, this may be the price that the other Churches or ethnic groups have paid for their lack of originality in the 1890s. Nonetheless, the 'brigades' set up some 80 years ago still deserve to be rescued from the almost complete oblivion of history. What justifies exploring them in more detail is that they were all called into existence — each with its own distinctive areas of recruitment — to solve differing problems of social adjustment or racial accommodation in late Victorian England. While on another level of correlated activity, they were also agencies developed by Evangelising middle-class adults to supervise and control the leisure of working-class adolescents.

The Church Lads' Brigade, which appeared in 1891 — eight years after its progenitor, the Boys' Brigade — proved to be the most numerically successful and long-surviving of all the rival organizations. Failing to recruit in the Boys' Brigade's traditional stronghold of Scotland, its main strength has always been in England, particularly in the cathedral cities of the South East.[1] The Church Lads' Brigade was the brain-child of Walter Mallock Gee.[2] Perhaps a less charismatic man than any of the youth leaders herein considered, he was an exhaustive

37

exponent of the necessity for juvenile temperance work among the young. In fact, the links between the formation of the Church Lads' Brigade and the temperance movement within the Church of England are crucial to an understanding of both its persistent early difficulties and the politics of the compromise solution which eventually overcame them. For without the help of the Church of England Temperance Society, 'it would have been very difficult to launch the work at all.'[3] From 1889, Gee himself was the Secretary of the CETS Junior Division, in which capacity he strongly urged Sunday School teachers to take up the Band of Hope.[4] Understandably, given these commitments, Gee was foremost among those Anglicans seeking to retain a 'hold' over those boys grown too old for Sunday School or Band of Hope and yet still too young to be able to join the adult temperance society.

Learning of the existence of the Boys' Brigade from one of the CETS police court missionaries[5] (the forerunners of the modern probationary service), Gee took it as his model of an organization for boys after they had graduated from CETS Bands of Hope. Like William Smith, his erstwhile mentor, Gee was a proud member of the Volunteers, which may explain his enthusiasm for the military method and its whole-hearted adoption by the Church Lads' Brigade.[6] Subsequently, this over-militarization did much to effectively damage their long-term prospects as a movement in the twentieth century. At the outset, Smith in Glasgow rejected the feasibility of an Anglican section working separately within the Boys' Brigade. And so, rather impetuously, on 23 July 1891, Gee decided to inaugurate his first Church Lads' Brigade Company at St Andrew's Parish Church in Fulham. He did this with the full backing of the incumbent, the Revd E. S. Hilliard, but without the blessing of the Boys' Brigade's national executive.[7]

The arguments for or against the 'sectarian' step taken by Gee in raising a 'brigade' exclusively for the Church of England need not detain us here. For the initial obstacles to the scheme did not emerge, as might be expected, from a disgruntled Boys' Brigade, but from within the Church of England temperance movement itself. Ironically, the case Gee had put for Anglican autonomy in order to convince the Boys' Brigade was now to be applied against his own organization. Thus, in the early 1890s, the Church Lads' Brigade failed in its initial bid to gain the support of influential clergymen, such as Dr Temple, the Bishop of London, who would have preferred a separatist movement along *total* abstinence lines. After protracted negotiations, this resulted in a schism: in deference to the Bishop's wishes, the London Diocesan Church Lads' Brigade was set up — and it continued in an independent existence, confined to the London Diocese, until 1919.[8] Disregarding ecclesiastical politics, Gee went ahead to convene the first public inaugural meeting of the Church Lads' Brigade; this was held on a wet day in November 1891 at Church House, Westminster, with the founder seen 'struggling blindly down the Westminster Bridge Road in vain search for a photographer.'[9]

In 1892, having successfully survived these internecine disputes, Gee agreed to become the first full-time Secretary of the Church Lads' Brigade. His resignation from the CETS post was made possible by a gift of £250 from Leonard Noble, who was thus well qualified to become the Brigade's first Honorary Treasurer.[10] Characteristically, Gee only accepted the position on condition that power within the Brigade was to be centralized for, as he put it: 'if I thought this could not be carried out, I should not for one moment think of taking the risk I am.'[11] The movement at first lacked support among prominent Bishops, apart from Winnington-Ingram, a future Bishop of London. In 1893 the Archbishop of Canterbury even went so far as to become a patron of their Nonconformist rival, the Boys' Brigade. Significantly, backing from the English military caste was much more forthcoming, and Lord Chelmsford, who in 1893 became the first Governor of the Brigade, was also the first in a long line of high-ranking army officers to fill the post.[12] The military organization and government of the Church Lads' Brigade was consolidated in 1892 when the Governing Brigade Council was established.[13] By 1897 every diocese in England and Wales was represented in the movement, although there was only one company in the whole of Scotland.

At the time the Boy Scouts were launched in 1908, there were, in total, 67 regiments, 118 battalions, over 1,300 companies and around 70,000 boys enrolled in the Church Lads' Brigade. To meet the competitive threat presented by Baden-Powell's new youth movement, the Brigade attempted half-heartedly to duplicate the success of the Scouts by setting up their own independent version of Scouting: the Incorporated Church Scout Patrols.[14] Despite such innovations, the Church Lads' Brigade never really succeeded in reaching the 'rougher' elements of juvenile society. Like the Band of Hope movement, it recruited chiefly not from the children of the very poor but from the operative or artisan class – the sons of skilled workers.[15] One deterrent to the low-paid, unskilled who may have wished to join the Brigade was the financial commitment that membership demanded.[16] While the Brigade's pool of recruitment was certainly linked with Church attendance, which was the cause and which the effect it is difficult to determine.

Normative values likely to appeal to the upwardly aspiring – sobriety, thrift, self-help, punctuality, obedience – were positively stressed in Brigade handbooks: 'Remember that the CLB aims at all its members being gentlemen.'[17] The obverse of this rather patronizing stress on middle-class behavioural norms was a consequent denigration of working-class life and 'street culture':

> Left to themselves in their leisure hours they are too apt to lounge about the streets, idling and imitating the language and habits of men ten years their seniors, and this at an age when their wealthier brothers are enjoying the free and healthy life of a Public School or College.[18]

The Brigade was publicized as providing a public-school surrogate for the working-class boy, stressing *esprit de corps* and the norms of militarism. The English middle-class origins of their Christian manliness ethic became the most apparent in comparison to the Boys' Brigade.

In general, as well as being more caught up with the temperance issue, the Church Lads' Brigade was more conformist, more militarized and more nationalistic than its Scottish counterpart – as its response to the Boer War amply demonstrated.[19] The features distinguishing the two major 'brigades' were even more clearly outlined in the years leading up to the First World War. Of crucial importance for their future development was that – unlike the Boys' Brigade – the Church Lads' Brigade chose, in 1911, to accept the Army Council's recommendation to apply to their local Territorials for official recognition as cadets. The Brigade's Annual Council succumbed in this way to a State imperative without much show of resistance, largely under the influence of the advice received from the pro-conscriptionist national executive.[20] In effect, the Church Lads' Brigade had virtually abandoned their religious objectives and were to remain by far the largest unit of the national cadet force for 25 years. This decision had not only exacerbated internal strains between religious and military factions within the Brigade but, with hindsight, can be seen as a strategic error that ultimately led to their identification in the public mind with military recruitment.

Thus the decline in the membership of the Church Lads' Brigade throughout the inter-war period can, with some credibility, be associated with their divergence from the Boys' Brigade before 1914 in pursuing the military means rather than the ostensibly religious ends. With the result that 'although many lads desired to join, they were prevented by parents, who imagined the CLB synonymous with militarism.'[21] The complacency of the Brigade's superannuated military leadership in the 1920s, when anti-militarist feeling was at its height, certainly revealed a lack of radical reforming energies. There was a marked absence of any ability to adjust to a rapidly changing post-war society. The Revd H. F. Peerless did his best to completely re-organize the Brigade when he took over as General Secretary in 1935, attempting to make it more a part of the Church and less military in every way. An endeavour after the Second World War to abolish uniform in favour of equipment (cap, belt and haversack), as favoured by the Boys' Brigade, failed; but Peerless re-wrote the Constitution and abol-ished the old Governing Body in favour of a democratically elected Brigade Council.[22] Before the advent of Peerless, there was a general failure to re-orientate the Brigade's policies on a competitive level with other youth movements. This meant that their ultimate with-drawal from cadet affiliation in 1936 — in effect demilitarizing the style of the CLB — came too late to prevent them from slipping into the position of a relatively small and uninfluential rival to the Boys' Brigade. A position which they have done little to improve upon to the present day.[23]

Another symptom of the hold the 'brigade' idea had upon potent-ial youth workers in the 1890s is the Jewish Lads' Brigade. While never aspiring to rival the membership of the Boys' Brigade or the Church Lads' Brigade,[24] it is of some interest for the light it sheds, in retro-spect, on both the immigrant Jewish community and the host nation. The driving force behind the setting up of the Jewish Lads' Brigade was Colonel Albert Edward Goldsmid,[25] an Anglo-Jewish, self-confessed 'Daniel Deronda' figure. Although a Zionist as well as an Anglophile, he made a successful career as a staff officer in the British Army. The idea for the Brigade came to Goldsmid while, as Colonel-in-Command at Cardiff, he was inspecting a local company of the Church Lads' Brigade.[26] Thus one imitator of the original Boys' Brigade model — the Church Lads' Brigade — became instrumental in the creation of another — the Jewish Lads' Brigade. The boys that Goldsmid intended to reach, however, were completely different in both religious and social composition from those Protestant youths catered for by his predecessors. His targets were the sons of Jewish immigrants crowding into the East End of London from the ghettoes of Poland and Russia.[27] Goldsmid genuinely wanted to help the poor Jewish boys his Zionist work in the East End had brought him into contact with, but there was also the added bonus that the Jewish Lads'

Brigade would keep boys out of mischief after they had left Board
School, and before they were old enough to join the Jewish Working
Men's Club or the newly emerging Jewish Boys' Club.

In 1894, Goldsmid delivered a lecture advocating the establishment
of a Jewish Lads' Brigade, along the lines of the Church Lads' Brigade,
to the Maccabeans. This was a society of English Jewish intellectuals,
professional men and artists, who held meetings and gave dinners for
the avowed purpose of arousing an interest in Jewish culture.[28] Although
at first hesitant, the Maccabeans were to provide most of the early
financial support and administrative supervision for the Brigade,[29]
whose inaugural meeting was held in February 1895 in the hall of the
Jews' Free School in Spitalfields.[30] Over 120 boys were present, drawn
in about equal proportions from pupils of the Jews' Hospital, apprent-
ices under the care of the Jewish Board of Guardians and boys from
East End Schools.[31] Most of the early companies were, however,
recruited chiefly from Jewish Board Schools within a mile radius of
Aldgate East.[32] For it was not really until the 1900s — with the
gradual dispersal of the Jewish community — that the Jewish Lads'
Brigade spread out into other areas of London. From 1913 Camper-
down House in Whitechapel was retained as the Brigade's social centre.
Officially, only Jewish officers were allowed in the Brigade, and
even these were strictly vetted for their social respectability.[33] Until
the Brigade started to recruit from within its own ranks of N.C.O.s,
there was a wide gulf separating boys — often speaking a foreign language — from their Anglo-Jewish, upper-middle-class officers. One old
man recalled acting as interpreter for his Russian father when two
Maccabean Captains came to his home about camp expenses. 'They
were English gentlemen of course, and when they had gone my father
asked, "They're Jewish?" '[34]

One lasting function of the Jewish Lads' Brigade was to facilitate
the racial integration — if not the assimilation — of Jewish immigrant
boys living in East End ghettoes into the 'host' English community.[35]
The Brigade, that is, acted as some sort of a mediator between the immigrant Jewish community and the English 'way of life' outside of the
ghetto. An instrument for the 'Anglicization' of the 'narrow chested,
round-shouldered, slouching son of the Ghetto', who, it was promised,
would become 'converted with extraordinary rapidity into an erect and
self-respecting man, a living negation of the physical stigma which has
long disfigured our race.'[36] Thus the Brigade enthusiastically promulgated the public-school 'ethic' as part of a self-evidently desirable
'English tradition'.[37] At the same time, the debate over the wisest

political strategy for achieving the Jewish State in Palestine was equally a part of the historical framework within which the setting up of the Brigade has to be understood.[38] It is hard to accept, nonetheless, that a pseudo-military organization, however much it may try to adjust its image, can be the most appropriate instrument of Jewish social and leisure education for a generation that is less subservient to self-consciously English patterns of authority than previous generations. A Jewish Girls' Brigade was not started until as late as 1963.[39]

Little is known about the next 'brigade' to be considered: the Catholic Boys' Brigade. Even its demise appears to be shrouded in obscurity. At least this much is clear: it was started in September 1896 at a boys' club in Bermondsey, the Dockland Students' Institute, by the local Catholic curate in charge, as a means of 'stemming the great tide of leakage from the Church.'[40] The Revd Father Felix Segesser,[41] a busy hard-working parish priest, born of a noble Austrian-Swiss father and an English mother, ran the club in connection with his evening continuation classes. He decided to form so-called 'cadets' in order to build up a juvenile membership which drew heavily upon the sons of a largely unskilled or semi-skilled Irish Catholic workforce in this predominantly dockland parish of South East London.[42] The idea of military training soon caught on with the boys, who drilled with sticks or broom handles before graduating to rifles – parading in cap, brown belt and haversack. Here again there is the same mixture of military drill and religion, physical exercises and ambulance classes, sports and camping. Later, a red and green uniform, symbolizing England and Ireland, was appropriately adopted after Father Segesser had unwillingly rejected the idea of imitating the Zouaves' uniform of the Papal Guard in Rome.[43]

This nucleus of 'cadets' in Bermondsey was originally called the South London Catholic Brigade, after the South London Catholic League, since the work was not expected to leave the parish. But the idea caught on among other Catholics and, despite the difficulty of getting a drill instructor, Father Newton in Rotherhithe, another dockland parish, started his own company, to be followed rapidly by others. The Brigade's main strength was always in London, with two battalions of 40 companies in the Winchester and Southwark Dioceses. One authority gives a membership total in 1906 of 8,000, of which at least half were in Ireland.[44] Segesser himself saw the main function of the Catholic Boys' Brigade as keeping Catholic adolescents true to the Church. A method of safeguarding their faith and morals after they had left school and before they could be reached by either the Society

of St Vincent de Paul or the Catholic Young Men's Society. The officers
of the Brigade appear to have been drawn either from the ranks of the
latter Society or from the Catholic Settlements Association.[45] While
funds lasted, Brigade camps were held regularly in Surrey.[46] In the late
1900s the Brigade came under increasingly hostile attack for its alleged
militarism, lay support evaporated and the movement began to show
all the signs of imminent collapse. After the First World War, the
Catholic Boys' Brigade is no longer mentioned in *The Catholic Directory*
and it appears to have been subsumed within the Catholic Boy Scouts
sometime in the 1920s.

The Boys' Life Brigade was started in the autumn of 1899 by the
Revd John Brown Paton[47] because of the antagonism which the
Boys' Brigade's military method had aroused among some Nonconformist Churchmen. 'Personally, I do not obejct to the military form of
the Boys' Brigade,' Paton confessed, 'but it is useless to ignore the fact
that many people do.'[48] Paton, the recently retired Principal of the
Nottingham Congregational Institute, was well qualified to judge their
efficacy, having taken a great interest in Boys' Brigade companies
both in Nottingham and Rugby. The immediate inspiration for the
new variation of a 'Life' brigade came to Paton from an old student:
the Revd T. A. Leonard of Colne, Lancashire. In 1897 he had started
a corps of Boys' Life Guards along non-military lines at his local Sunday
School.[49] Paton then brought the concept up before the National
Sunday School Union, a Nonconformist movement often critical of
the Boys' Brigade, and persuaded them to adopt it as a national organization with himself as the first President. Accordingly, until its dis-
bandment 27 years later, the Boys' Life Brigade was to remain an
integral part of the National Sunday School Union.

The Boys' Life Brigade was to embrace all the qualities Paton so
admired in the Boys' Brigade but without, as he put it, 'the least
tincture of militarism.'[50] The first company, called the 'Paton Company' after the President of the Brigade, was formed by a Major C. R.
Woodward in Nottingham.[51] The object of the Life Brigade was sought
chiefly, 'by means of drill which is not associated with the use of
arms, but with instruction and exercises in the saving of life from fire,
from drowning and from accident.'[52] Life saving drill, that is, was to
be used in the Boys' Life Brigade to give the obedience and discipline
which the Boys' Brigade claimed to instil, but without resort to the
military method that brought the latter into disrepute with a vocif-
erous section of Nonconformist opinion. By 1914 there were over
15,000 boys and 400 companies in the Life Brigade, mostly connected

with the English Free Churches. The Boys' Life Brigade merged with the Boys' Brigade in 1926, but only after some protracted and often acrimonious negotiations that had gone on intermittently since the First World War.[53] One concession made was that the Boys' Life Brigade's red-cross symbol formed the new amalgamated crest together with the Boys' Brigade's anchor, while the junior movements developed by both Brigades became known in future under the generic title of Life Boys.

That there was both a demand from boys for military drill in uniform and an adult willingness to provide for it before 1914 is also evident from the numerous, more short-lived 'brigades' established in the 1900s.[54] Unlike the movements considered so far, their membership rarely reached above the hundreds. Reference might also be made to such organizations as the Boys' Naval Brigade, a forerunner of the Sea Cadet Corps run by the Navy League, or to the London Newsboys' Brigade and many more in a similar mould.[55] The majority of these smaller 'brigades', such as the ubiquitous Boys' Rifle Brigades, were formed on free-enterprise lines by committed individuals. The idea itself was still both popular and resonant enough to make an appeal in the regional areas of Britain. But the prevalence of the 'military spirit' is alone insufficient to account for the various 'brigades' alluded to here. Demographic and economic changes at the turn of the century were conducive to the emergence of the concept of 'adolescence' and its gradual extension outside of the privileged classes, where a combination of low fertility with low mortality made a period of extended youth possible, even desirable.[56] The proliferation of 'brigades' suggests that, within the constraints of a short-term market demand for boy labour,[57] adults recognized more leisure time was now becoming available for the 'ordinary' working boy. Equally, parents were both more willing and financially able to see their sons' free time occupied in membership of a youth movement.

The particular Churches or ethno-religious groups involved feared the loss of their 'hold' over an age group at risk — the urban teenager:

> Of all physical exercises that can be used to allure and capture boys, to *hold* them fast and make them amenable to the finest discipline and some of the finest influences that can mould their character, [wrote J. B. Paton boldly] the best are found in the Boys' Brigades, which have happily now come into vogue.[58]

This in itself was one expression of a more general 'cycle of anxiety' concerning the behavioural problem of juvenile delinquency in urban society.[59] In London, it was also a period during which the socially responsible middle and upper-middle classes were being made more aware, through such sub-agencies as university settlements, public-school missions and boys' clubs, of how endemic poverty and 'dead-end' occupations were among the youth of the city.[60] 'Society was seized' wrote the journalist Henry Nevinson, 'by one of its brief and fitful fevers for doing good.'[61] In this climate of charitable concern, many public-school boys and university graduates found themselves enrolled as officers in a 'brigade' of some sort. These young men were reliant upon their drill-sergeant for the necessary expertise in military training and upon the local vicar for sufficient religious instruction to carry them through a Bible Class.

After the First World War, when there was a revulsion against anything 'military' among parents, the 'brigades' entered a trough from which only the Boys' Brigade made any appreciable recovery. In the case of the Church Lads' Brigade, the general public probably found it hard to determine until 1936 how it differed in practice from any other military cadet force.[62] During the inter-war period further historical and cultural trends were setting in against the 'brigade idea' which are more difficult to measure — such as, the decline of Christian manliness as a part of clerical homiletic, and a general relaxation of subordination to authority and regimentation in British society. In the 1950s and 1960s, the remaining brigades reflected a somewhat obsolescent, authoritarian mode of leadership which, unlike Scouting, did not take enough account of historical changes in the general style of relationship between adults and youth.[63] Uniformed parades and military drill no longer had the wide appeal they possessed in the 1890s: they were seen as boring, repetitive, dull, and progressively unrepresentative of modern teenage interests:

> If the Church Lads' Brigade is to remain an Anglican, uniformed, militarily structured, single sex organisation, [pointed out the Bishop of Exeter's Report sharply in 1966] it would be unrealistic in the prevailing moral and social climate, to expect it to make a broad-front appeal to boys.[64]

Addendum

The contribution of the Church Lads' Brigade and the Boys' Brigade to the war effort from 1914-1918 has been called a 'staggering achievement', considering that they began as voluntary organizations for less privileged boys in the cities. Cadet units of the CLB Training Corps were all affiliated to the King's Royal Rifle Corps and these alone formed the 16th Service Battalion of that Regiment and later its reserve battalion, the 19th (S.) Battn., KRRC. Altogether, over a quarter of a million ex-members of the CLB 'joined up' in the British forces. (See Edgar Rogers, *The Making of a Man in the C.L.B.* (London, 1919), p. viii.) The 16th Highland Light Infantry Battalion was raised entirely from among former members of the Glasgow Boys' Brigade, although they had difficulty at first in getting official recognition. (See Martin Middlebrook, *The First Day on the Somme* (London, 1971), p. 14.) These battalions were among those decimated on the Somme in 1916: the 16th (S.) Battn., KRRC suffered such heavy casualties that it ceased to exist as a battalion, while the Glasgow Boys' Brigade Battalion lost over five hundred men.

Notes

1. By 1910 there were 1,262 companies of the Church Lads' Brigade in England and Wales but only 9 in Scotland, most of them in Edinburgh. The majority of companies, outside the strongholds of London and Manchester, were in cathedral cities, such as Canterbury, Worcester, Exeter and Bath. Strong battalions could also be found in cities such as Cardiff and Liverpool.

2. Apart from his CETS work in the late 1880s, Gee was evidently an enthusiast who ate, drank and slept the CLB. In the self-effacing mould of William Smith, he is characterized as an unselfish, modest, dedicated worker who shunned publicity. Also like Smith, he was a Volunteer – a Captain in the 1st Volunteer Brigade of the Berkshire Regiment. See Gee's obituaries: *The Times*, 26 December 1916; the *Church Times*, 29 December 1916; *The Brigade*, Vol. XXIII, No. 2 (February 1917).

3. Anon., *Twentieth Anniversary Souvenir of the Church Lads' Brigade, 1891-1911* (London, 1911), p. 12. Cf. Lilian Shiman, 'The Church of England Temperance Society in the Nineteenth Century', *The Historical Magazine of the Protestant Episcopal Church*, Vol. XLI (June, 1972), pp. 179-195; Anon., *History and Work of the C.E.T.S.* (London, 1895), BM.

4. See W. M. Gee, 'The Sunday School and the Band of Hope' in *The Illustrated Temperance Monthly*, Vol. I (1891), pp. 97, 137, 208-209; *idem, The Nation's Hope: a practical text book for Band of Hope workers and all interested in the education and control of children* (London, 1891).

5. *Twentieth Anniversary Souvenir*, p. 2.

6. Whereas military ranks in the Boys' Brigade went no higher than Captain (William Smith's rank even as Founder), the Church Lads' Brigade adopted full military organization, terminology and instructional methods. Gee, for example, was listed in the Brigade List and Gazette of Commissions – closely modelled on Army practice – as a Colonel, late Captain in the

Volunteers. He is supposed to have spent many long days in the British Museum studying the whole history of the Volunteers in England.

7. The controversy over the timing of the setting up of the Church Lads' Brigade was revived in 1896 by the Dublin press. See private pamphlet, *Correspondence in the Dublin press re 'Boys' Brigade'*, October 1896, in author's private possession. It includes extracts from the June 1891 correspondence between Smith and Gee to confirm the latter's case.

8. See *Twentieth Century Souvenir*, pp. 5-11. The Secretary of the LDCLB was Everard Ford, Treasurer of the Lay Helpers' Association and a member of the London Diocesan Council. By 1906 the LDCLB numbered about 7,000 officers and boys, divided into 160-odd separate companies.

9. Ibid., p. 18.

10. Ibid., p. 24. Noble, whose gift really set the new 'brigade' on its feet financially, later served as a Major in the Imperial Yeomanry during the South African War, contributing a regular 'Letter of our Treasurer from the Front' to the CLB journal, *The Brigade.*

11. Cited, *loc. cit.* Although as modest and self-effacing as William Smith, at least in public, the evidence from Brigade Executive Committee Minutes tends to suggest that Gee could be autocratic and strong-willed when he thought it necessary.

12. Chelmsford became Governor on retiring from the Active List in 1893. Lord Methuen succeeded Chelmsford, serving from 1905 to 1908. One of the most incompetent generals in the South African War, in 1902 he even managed to be captured. From 1908 to 1925, the Governor was Lord Grenfell: Sirdar of the Egyptian Army, (1885-1892); Inspector-General of Auxiliary Forces at the War Office, (1894-1897); Inspector-General of Recruiting (1896); Commander-in-Chief Ireland (1904-1908). Both Methuen and Grenfell were Vice-Presidents of Lord Meath's Lads' Drill Association (1899-1906).

13. The Brigade Council comprised: the members of the Governing Body, none of whom were company officers; regimental Colonels and staff officers, who had to be regular or territorial soldiers; and one chaplain and one lay officer elected by each battalion, the latter usually a member of the battalion staff and also a territorial officer. Consequently, rank-and-file company officers or chaplains were under-represented at the Annual Council Conferences — which decided on major policy changes — while the military side was over-represented.

14. See *The I.C.S.P. Scout Message and Handicrafts for Boys, 1911-1914*; Paul Wilkinson, ' A study of English Uniformed Youth Movements, 1883-1935', M.A. thesis, University of Wales, 1968, pp. 50-52. The CLB's lack of any real enthusiasm for genuine 'woodcraft' activities is illustrated by this venture, which collapsed from insufficient executive level support.

15. See the evidence of Douglas Eyre, Chairman of the executive committee of the Federation of Working Lads' Clubs in London to the *Inter-Departmental Committee on Physical Deterioration*, PP, 1904 (Cd. 2210), Vol. XXXII, Mins. of Evidence, 3577, p. 153; *Membership of the Church Lads' Brigade*, a survey conducted on behalf of the Bishop of Exeter's Committee by Research Services Ltd. (London, February 1966), p. 3. The latter established that 55 per cent of the membership was drawn from the skilled working class.

16. Each boy had to pay 1s.6d. on entrance in the mid-1900s, and a penny a week towards the general funds, as well as 2d. a week towards a seaside camp. See Anon. (Reginald Hennell), *Our Birthright* (London, 1906), p. 20. Most shop boys and errand boys would earn only a few shillings

a week: see Spencer J. Gibb, *The Problem of Boy Work* (London, 1906), chap. 2.

17. Anon., *Guide for Company Officers, Warrant Officers and Privates of the Church Lads' Brigade* (CLB, 1933), p. 6; the following advice is also given: 'Be punctual in all your payments . . . Never holloa and make a noise in the streets . . . Never use bad language . . . Be careful never to spit . . . Never throw orange peel or banana skins on the pavement.' Ibid., pp. 16-17. Cf. *The Church Lads' Brigade Training Corps Guide*, (CLB, 1916), pp. 21-22.

18. Anon., *General Objects C.L.B. Fifth Annual Report, 1896/1897*, n.p. For a contrary view of working-class adolescent 'street culture', cf. Robert Roberts, *The Classic Slum: Salford life in the first quarter of the century* (London, Pelican edn., 1973), pp. 155-157; Howard Parker, *View from the Boys* (London, 1974).

19. E.g., one editorial claimed that 'every member of the CLB must feel proud of the fact that such a large number of its members have been chosen for active service at the Front.' *The Brigade*, Vol. VI (January, 1900), p. 13. CLB members were also encouraged to join the Volunteers, with whom they frequently paraded during the war in South Africa. See *The Brigade*, Vol. VI (March, 1900), p. 59.

20. See Reports of the Annual Council Meetings, 11-12 May 1911, Special Supplement, in *The Brigade*, Vol. XVII, No. 7 (July, 1911), pp. 13-21; several members of this executive, including Gee, had spoken at meetings of the National Service League in support of conscription.

21. F. G. Marshall, *St. Mary Lewisham Church Lads' Brigade, 1892-1929* (London, 1930), p. 24. Marshall also says: 'From 1919 to 1924, the Company undoubtedly passed through a very difficult period.' Ibid.

22. See obituary in *The Brigade*, Vol. LXXXII, No. 3 (July, 1975), p. 18; and taped interviews with: J. Veysey, Captain St Mary, Lewisham, 1935-1960, recorded 20 September 1971; A. J. Ormiston, Captain, St. Margaret's Co., Twickenham, recorded 15 September 1971.

23. From 1955 to 1965, the membership of the CLB declined by 26 per cent, i.e. from 16, 245 to 11,944. The latest figures available, for 1973, give them a boy strength of 8,879 in 320 units; whereas the British Isles total for the Boys' Brigade amounts to 140,500, including their Junior Section. I am grateful fo CLB Staff Officer Ken Buxton for supplying me with reliable up-to-date statistics on membership.

24. Figures supplied by the JLB in the early 1900s suggest a membership of just over 1,000 boys in London and 4,000 throughout England; although one work claims that the highest enrolment reached was perhaps only 1,000 to 1,500. See Lloyd P. Gartner, *The Jewish Immigrant in England, 1870-1914* (London, 1973 edn.), p. 174.

25. A. E. Goldsmid (1846-1904). See Biographical Notes.

26. Goldsmid was so impressed by their performance that he remarked to his daughter, the future Lady Swaythling, that 'something similar should be arranged for our Jewish lads'. Cited in Charles A. Magnus, *E.M.J.*, (Ernest M. Joseph), (London, 1962), p. 33. Goldsmid became a Vice-President of the CLB.

27. In general, their fathers would be: upholsterers, tailors, shoemakers and dealers in furs; largely from streets such as: Gravel Lane, Brady Street, Old Castle Street and Chicksand Street, in Whitechapel, east of Aldgate, with some towards Houndsditch, of Dutch Jewish extraction. See taped interview with M. Robins, Secretary JLB, recorded at the Brady Street Club, Whitechapel, 22 October 1973.

28. See Olga Somech Phillips, *The Maccabeans* (n.d. 1927?), leaflet in the Mocatta Library, University College, London; Professor Norman Bentwich, 'The Wanderers and other Jewish Scholars of my Youth' in *Transactions of the Jewish Historical Society of England, 1959-1961* (London, 1964), Vol. XX, pp. 56-57; Marvin Lowenthal (ed.), *The Diaries of Theodor Herzl*, (London, 1958), p. 81, p. 176; Chaim Bermant, *Troubled Eden: an anatomy of British Jewry* (London, 1969), p. 34.

29. Even as late as 1899, out of 14 members of the JLB's Executive Committee, nine were also Maccabeans; including their Secretary, Dr. B. L. Abrahams, a consulting physician at University College Hospital. See *List of Members*, Maccabean Society, 1895, 1900, Mocatta Library, op. cit. In the 1890s, the 'Maccabean Company' of the Jews' Free School Battalion was one of the largest in the JLB.

30. The Jews' Free School in Bell Lane, Spitalfields, had over 3,500 Jewish pupils. A Board of Trade Report of 1904 declared that it was one of the most powerful instruments for Anglicizing the foreign Jewish community in London. According to this Report, 'they enter the School Russians and Poles and emerge from it almost indistinguishable from English children'. Cited in V. D. Lipman, *A Social History of the Jews in England, 1850-1950* (London, 1954), p. 146.

31. See Sidney Bunt, *Jewish Youth Work in Britain: past, present, and future* (London, 1975), p. 165. I am grateful to Mr Bunt, Education and Training Officer of the National Association of Youth Clubs, for allowing me to see his book in typescript.

32. E.g., by 1898 there were 35 boys in the Deal Street JLB Company drawn from a new Jewish School in Mile End New Town whose Headmaster described the JLB as 'an admirable movement for developing the physique, for inculcating habits of obedience and self-restraint and for fostering a spirit of true patriotism'. Cited in Examination of Joseph P. Rawden, *Royal Commission on Alien Immigration*, Mins. of Evidence, Cd. 1742, Vol. IX, 1903, 18873.

33. A Jewish bill discounter and a bookmaker were not considered to be sufficiently 'socially desirable' by the JLB Executive Committee. See Minutes of the Executive Committee, 5 April, 1898; 21 September 1899: Books 1-2, AJ 34/11/17, Mocatta Library, op. cit.

34. Cited in Anon., 'The JLB . . . How It Came About' in *The Jewish Chronicle J.L.B. Supplement*, 27 October 1972, p. ii.

35. Thus, when 500 JLB boys were subjected to a census during the 1902 Camp at the Sandhills, Deal, Kent, it was found that over 75 per cent of them were of foreign parentage and many of them were born abroad, but 'they looked just like English boys. That is most remarkable.' Examination of Jack M. Myers, *Royal Comm.*, op. cit., 818.

36. Anon., 'The Jewish Lads' Brigade', leaflet (n.d. 1897?), p. 2, reprinted from *The Jewish Chronicle*, Mocatta Library, op. cit.

37. See. Louis Golding, *The Sixtieth Anniversary of the Jewish Lads' Brigade* (London, 1954), n.p. For Golding, a distinguished former member, this 'tradition' included: 'a willing acceptance of authority', 'fair play' and '*esprit de corps*'.

38. Goldsmid, a self-declared 'nationalist Jew' was the British Chief of Chovevi Zion, a Zionist organization, which expressed a traditional, albeit platonic, sympathy for the resettlement of Jews in Palestine. Despite their pilgrimages to Palestine, the Maccabeans and Goldsmid were not militant enough for Theodor Herzl, a founding father of the Jewish State. See Virginia Cowles, *The Rothschilds* (London, 1973), pp. 192-193; Walter

Laqueur, *A History of Zionism* (London, 1972), chap. 3; Marvin Lowenthal (ed.), *The Diaries of Theodor Herzl* (London, 1958), pp. 82-83.

39. The Jewish Girls' Brigade is, in reality, the JLB modified, with first aid, basketry, cooking and handicrafts to supplement the military drill. The two 'brigades' still function separately, except for ceremonial or special occasions. See Sidney Bunt, *Jewish Youth Work*, p. 166.

40. Cited in *The Universe*, 4 June 1909, p. 11. It is pointed out here that a study was made of 'brigades' outside of the Catholic Church before the scheme was initiated, although another source denies the idea was copied from elsewhere.

41. F. Segesser (1863-1930). See Biographical Notes.

42. See Anon., 'The Catholic Boys' Brigade: its origins and growth' in *Plum Duff*, a quarterly magazine, Vol. I, No. 1 (October, 1905), p. 16, BM.

43. Loc. cit. At first, the boys in this touch dockside area were not all keen to be seen in public in unoform; so they compromised by coming along to the Club bringing their uniforms wrapped up in brown paper and changing on arrival.

44. See Anon. (Reginald Hennell), *Our Birthright* (London, 1906), p. 21.

45. The Catholic Settlements Association was a body of Catholic laymen from leading Catholic colleges, working in Hoxton, the Borough and South London generally; the Catholic Young Men's Society was the Catholic equivalent of the YMCA.

46. In 1909 there were 900 boys present at Camp in Effingham, Surrey, making up three battalions of the Brigade. George Pauling, who edited *Plum Duff*, provided the land and subscribed £100 of his own to the Brigade; but the Camp itself cost six times as much, leaving the deficit in Camp funds to be met by Brigade staff members. See Ninth Annual Report CBB cited in *The Catholic Boys' Brigade Gazette*, Vol. I, No. 2 (July, 1910), p. 5.

47. J. L. Paton (1830-1911). See biographies appended.

48. Cited in John Lewis Paton, *John Brown Paton: a biography by his son* (London, 1914), p. 315.

49. Ibid., p. 313. Leonard has been described as the 'father of the open-air movement' in England. See David Prynn, 'The Clarion Clubs, Rambling and the Holiday Associations in Britain since the 1890s', *Journal of Contemporary History*, 71 (1976), p. 71.

50. Ibid., p. 329

51. One of the strongest companies in the BLB was in Eastwood, D. H. Lawrence's birthplace, a mining village near Nottingham, where first-aid and fire drill had a readily recognizable value. Ibid., p. 316.

52. Anon., *Code of Rules and Regulations*, Boys' Life Brigade (BLB, 1900) p. 6. BM.

53 There is a large correspondence, of often Byzantine complexity and deviousness, dealing with these negotiations at the Boys' Brigade Headquarters in London. One file deals with 1914, the other with 1920-1926. The prospects for amalgamation were improved when, in 1924, the Boys' Brigade took the opportunity to cut all remaining ties with the War Office cadet scheme and passed a resolution to discard the use of the rifle.

54. E.g., an Imperial Lads' Brigade was started in West Hartepool in 1908, for 14 to 21 year olds, with drill and a rifle club, never exceeding 250 members, 'to make good citizens and loyal subjects, and to encourage lads to live better and purer lives.' Cf. C.E.B. Russell and L. M. Rigby, *Working Lads' Clubs* (London, 1908), pp. 323-324. In 1911, James Ickringill, a Primitive Methodist mill-owner living in Keighley, near Bradford,

started his own Good Lads' Brigade, requiring compulsory attendance at the local mission Sunday School hall. Cf. Almond, comp., *Biography of James Ickringill Esq* (Keighley, 1919), chap. 5. I am grateful to my colleague, Steve Ickringill, for drawing this to my attention.

55.   See Alicia Percival, *Youth will be Led* (London, 1951), p. 139; Reginald Hennell, p. 22.

56.   See F. Musgrove, *Youth and the Social Order* (London, 1964), chap. 4.

57.   See Gareth Stedman Jones, *Outcast London* (Oxford, 1971), pp. 68-71; Reginald Bray, *Boy Labour and Apprenticeship* (London, 1911), pp. ʼ14-118.

58.   J. L. Paton, p. 329.

59.   See John R. Gillis, 'The Evolution of Juvenile Delinquency in England, 1890-1914' in *Past and Present*, No. 67 (May, 1975), pp. 96-126.

60.   In the 1890s over a dozen largely University sponsored residential settlements were set up in London working-class areas, viz., Cambridge House (1888/90), Mansfield House University Settlement (1890), Oxford and Bermondsey Club (1897), Bermondsey Settlement (1891), and Browning Settlement (1890).

61.   Henry Nevinson, *Changes and Chances* (London, 1923), p. 78.

62.   But it was not compulsory for the CLB to take cadet training or to become affiliated, so that during the 1930s a gradual seepage of numbers occurred as each year detachments revoked their membership. Whereas in 1931 there were some 20,000 cadets in the CLB, or about one third of their total units, only about 4,000 boys were affected in 1936 when the final withdrawal came. Some units of the CLB broke away when this decision was reached, formed their own association as the British Lads' Brigade, and re-applied for affiliation to the BNCA, but little more was heard of them. See Anon., 'The Cadet Story, 1860-1960', Part VIII, *The Cadet Journal* (June, 1960), p. 124.

63.   See Fred Milson, *Youth Work in the 1970s* (London, 1970), pp. 44-45; John Gillis, *Youth and History* (London, 1974), chap. 10; John Wakelin, *et el, Responsibility for Youth* (London, 1961), Bow Group pamphlet; *The Albermarle Committee on Youth Service in England and Wales* (London, 1960), Cmd. 929, HMSO, para. 138.

64.   The Bishop of Exeter's Committee, *Church Lads' Brigade Report*, 1966, p. 17.

3 PLAYING THE GAME

'There can never be another discoverer of Scouting', points out one
biographer of Baden-Powell, 'any more than there can ever be a second
founder of Christianity.'[1] While no other British youth movement is
so manifestly the embodiment of its founder's personal vision as
Scouting, it was as much the product of an era or of the national
culture as of any one man. To explore the relationship between the
versatile Baden-Powell's life and the wider framework within which he
tried to give some shape to his personal experience, is to clarify why and
how the Boy Scouts came into existence.

Born in 1857 into a well-connected, professional middle-class
family, Robert Stephenson Smyth Powell (the Baden was subsequently
added, hyphenated, and in 1869 legalized for the whole family), was
probably more attached than his brothers to their mother, Henrietta
Grace Smyth. This was a relationship of intense devotion, and it endured
into his marriage when he was in his mid-fifties. It was the family
competitiveness which she inspired in her sons, as much as anything
else, that drove them on to success in their various careers.[2] Outside
the family circle, the most formative influences on the young Baden-
Powell's outlook were supplied by the corporate ethic of institutions,
particularly his public school and the British Army. In 1870 he was
sent to Charterhouse School on a Gownboy Foundationer Scholarship.[3] Like Winston Churchill at Harrow, Baden-Powell had a poorish
academic record, but the open-air individualism of the school's Head-
master, the Revd William Haig-Brown,[4] did much to determine his
future moral values. While at Charterhouse, Baden-Powell was a great
'joiner' of schoolboy societies and clubs, such as the embryonic rifle
corps. Yet this exuberant, extrovert side to his schoolboy nature was
balanced by a certain aloofness and lack of close friendships.[5]

Above all, as a schoolboy, Baden-Powell unequivocally accepted the
need to conform, to rejoice in the public-school 'code' of Charterhouse;
which was, perhaps, to find its ultimate expression in the Scout Law and
Promise.[6] The key words of the old Scout Law —honour, loyalty and
duty — were the emotional moulds within which British public-school
attitudes set. 'The principle of the public school discipline of "good
form" and "playing the game", ' Baden-Powell declared much later,
'needs developing along the right lines and extension to [the] other

ranks of life.'[7] It was not entirely fortuitous that the Boy Scouts were
the instrument chosen for 'trying to teach some of the Public School
spirit and tone to the elementary schoolboy.'[8] For Scouting is one
of the most obvious twentieth-century products of a general tendency
in English life to reject disdainfully the unhealthy vulgarity of capitalist
urban-industrial values, and this tendency goes back at least as far
as the Christian Socialism of the mid-nineteenth century. In *Tom
Brown' Schooldays* (1857), Thomas Hughes has even been accused of
transforming Dr Arnold of Rugby into a 'glorified [boy] Scoutmaster
whose strenuous spirituality has been made palatable to Englishmen by
presenting it under the guise of the honest manliness of a [Charles]
Kingsley hero.'[9] Hughes helped to bring into being the nineteenth-
century public-school ethos of 'muscular Christianity', which upheld
the moral and physical value of 'masculine' games as opposed to
'effeminate' and intellectual scholarship.[10] And the Boy Scouts inherited the pastoral 'myth' of open air woodcraft, with its conviction
that Nature symbolized the greatest available purity; together with the
paternalistic longing for class harmony and collaboration in rural sports
evident in Christian Socialism.

While the traditions of the Victorian public school were central to
the basic philosophy behind Scouting, Baden-Powell's long career as
a professional soldier was equally germane. It not only provided material
for the famous Boy Scout handbook but also gave him many of the
over-simplified responses to complex social and political problems of
the English military mind. Baden-Powell further claimed that Scouting
was no sudden inspiration, but rather 'a mixture of experiences gradually gathered in training recruits in the Army.'[11] So whether he is
portrayed as 'one of the greatest generals of modern times',[12] or as 'a
somewhat ridiculous and vain little colonel',[13] Baden-Powell's out-
standingly adventurous military experiences in India and Africa must
have provided the touchstone for many of the elements that went
into the making of the Boys Scouts. Not that Baden-Powell was by any
standards a conventional army officer. He sat an open examination for
his commission and, after the curious contemporary War Office practice, was excused Sandhurst because of the successful result. Perhaps
because he never went to Staff College, Baden-Powell always retained a
suspicion of formal, orthodox military training. Nowhere is this better
expressed than in his injunction to Scoutmasters not to adopt military
drill in training the Boy Scout, since, in his opinion, it destroyed
individuality and merely gave 'a feeble unimaginative officer a something with which to occupy his boys.'[14]

It is a paradox that a movement like Scouting, which has become so much an integral part of the British Establishment scene, should have been founded by a soldier who inveighed against the unimaginative tedium which represented military training in the late Victorian army. Baden-Powell was also unusual as an army officer in that he liked to draw caricatures, to do imitations of senior officers, to act in amateur theatricals and to play practical jokes. His nephew, Donald, once wrote: 'I have often thought what a wonderful actor or producer he could have made.'[15] Despite all his drive and enthusiasm, Baden-Powell was aware of the doubts his high-spirited conduct often raised among his staider colleagues: 'It does upset some of their notions of the gravity expected of a full colonel,' he exclaimed on taking over the command of the 5th Dragoon Guards in India, 'that I play polo and go pig-sticking whenever I can make the chance.'[16] While young and eager for promotion, he even found the time to publish several army manuals, a book on pig-sticking and accounts of the Matabele and Ashanti campaigns which he had personally witnessed as a soldier in Africa.[17] Like the equally irrepressible and ambitious Winston Churchill, the future Chief Scout sought to distinguish himself professionally at this stage in his career. But it was not until the Boer War at the turn of the century that a providential occasion appeared with which his name was to become indelibly linked: the siege of Mafeking.

The merits of the opposing arguments on whether Baden-Powell's mobile frontier force was meant to garrison the town at all,[18] or how carefully calculated and skilfully concealed his motives may have been, cannot be considered here. But there can be little doubt that it was his inventive, resourceful and highly publicized defence during the famous siege that ultimately brought him a notoriety which he occasionally regretted. The news also arrived at a time when the hard pressed British needed a hero to redeem a series of humiliating defeats suffered at the hands of the Boer guerillas. Mafeking and all that it came to symbolize became a part of the Baden-Powell legend. One of the final things Baden-Powell had done before leaving England was to deliver the manuscript of his most recent army instruction manual, *Aids to Scouting for N.C.O.'s and Men*, to the publishers. The proofs were in the last of the letters to get through the Boer lines before Mafeking was beseiged. Like a time-bomb quietly ticking away, a manual intended for soldiers was taken up by youth workers and teachers. This set Baden-Powell thinking about adapting it for boys.[19]

Once the famous siege was over, Baden-Powell was made Inspector-General of the South African Constabulary. By now a neat little Major-

General in his early forties, he performed the office with his customary strenuous efficiency. In 1901 over-exertion led to his being ordered home on sick-leave, where he was received as a hero. Then, early in 1903, he was offered the position of Inspector-General of Cavalry.An appointment which suggested to some that Whitehall harboured a certain resentment against the further promotion of such an egregious soldier. 'The bright fruition of fortune and success was soon obscured by a chilly fog', in Winston Churchill's declamatory phrase.[20] When his term of duty ended in 1907, Baden-Powell was placed on half-pay with the rank of a Lieutenant-General. Adventitiously, the new Minister of Defence in the Liberal Government, R. B. Haldane, offered him the command of the Northumbrian Division of the recently formed Territorials. Baden-Powell held this post until 1910, when he chose to resign and devote himself full-time to the Boy Scouts.[21]

What led up to Baden-Powell's decision to abandon his army career when, at the age of 53, the highest military ranks were, theoretically, still open to him? Quite sensibly, he wanted to dissociate the Boy Scouts in the public mind from the Territorials.[22] More important, the crucial commitment to his new career resulted from a fear of the degeneration of the young and for the survival of the British Empire which they would have to maintain:

> In the next generation there should be no overgrown lads standing idly and foolishly at the street corners, gaping after they know not what, smoking cigarettes, [wrote one admirer of the new youth movement] there will be a new race of boys in England when the Scouts of today have little Scouts of their own.[23]

But why should this preoccupation with 'saving the rising generation rather than doctoring the old one'[24] have arisen more acutely in the 1900s than in any other period?

> *Now* is the time while enthusiasm is still warm and before we sink back into our English easy chair [wrote Baden-Powell to his publisher] for us to prepare a wise and practical organization of the splendid material lying ready to our hand.[25]

Written at the time he was busy organizing the South African Constabulary, this suggests that the Boy Scouts were primarily intended to serve as a form of national preparation or long-term insurance against the recrudescence of the political and military incompetence Baden-

Powell came to identify with the Boer War.

One effect of the Boer War upon British politicians was its revelation
of the military weaknesses of the British Empire. To find explanations,
numerous Royal Commissions and Committees of Inquiry were set up
by the anxious authorities to investigate military inadequacies.[26]
'Recent reports on the deterioration of our race,' wrote Baden-Powell
ominously, 'ought to act as a warning to be taken in time before it
goes too far.'[27] Like many another social imperialist, Baden-Powell had
taken up the fashionable idea of 'deterioration' from a report on
'Physical Deterioration' which appeared in 1904; it was an idea which
soon became interchangeable with degeneracy or decadence. This added
an implication of moral decline to the fear of physical worsening —
which the report was in fact intended to refute.[28] That Baden-Powell
was susceptible to such half-truths can be seen from his reaction to
the social welfare reforms of Asquith's Liberal Government, whose
measures to combat poverty convinced him that 'over-civilisation'
threatened England with deterioration. 'Free feeding and old age
pensions, strike pay, cheap beer and indiscriminate charity,' he claimed,
'do not make for the hardening of the nation or the building up of a
self-reliant, energetic manhood.'[29] When asked in 1918 what his purpose
was in forming the Boy Scout organization, Baden-Powell replied in a
key document that it was 'to counteract if possible the deterioration
moral and physical which shortened our rising generation, and to train
the boys to be more efficient and characterful citizens.'[30]

Baden-Powell's aloof, brisk, slightly arrogant personality exuded a
patriotic earnestness. He believed that the threat of national decadence
was evident in both the supposed physical deterioration of the British
race and in the lack of enthusiasm for Empire. Such an outlook was
basic to Baden-Powell's diagnosis of the imperial condition after the
reverses suffered during the Boer War. It is hardly surprising that the
decline and fall of the Roman Empire should have been adopted as one
of his more favourite analogies.[31] One remedy to save Britain from the
fate of Rome was encapsulated in the concept of national efficiency,
which was among the most influential intellectual concepts in Edwardian
governing circles.[32] It united men of widely differing political allegian-
ces who often shared with Baden-Powell an impatience at the delays
and quarrels of British politics. The cult of efficiency, with its semi-
Prussian overtones, was so nebulous that it could appeal simultaneously
to radical Fabians and Tory imperialists. Baden-Powell was influenced
by this current trend for, in its way, Scouting was a response to the
demand for 'organizing' British youth as efficiently as possible.[33] It

is not entirely coincidental that Haldane, one of the foremost apostles of national efficiency, gave Baden-Powell the encouragement necessary to leave the Army and launch the Boy Scouts.

> I liked the Boy Scout, [wrote H. G. Wells approvingly in 1910] and I find it difficult to express how much it mattered to me, with my growing bias in favour of deliberate national training that Liberalism hadn't been able to produce, and had indeed never attempted to produce, anything of this kind.[34]

The climate of opinion in this period also gave popular currency to another major strand in Baden-Powell's intellectual armoury: social Darwinism.[35] Since the 1880s, a gradual shift in the aims of British youth had taken place, whereby ideologies of national purpose were effectively supplanting earlier religious and moral justifications, although the latter remained very much a part of public rhetoric.[36] And this new nationalist orientation was often couched in social Darwinist terms of racial survival. 'As each generation has come and gone,' pronounced an advocate of the Church Lads' Brigade, 'the intensified struggle for existence has been visible in a declining virility and a corresponding increase of the wastrel and degenerate.'[37] The idea of the 'survival of the fittest' among nations engaged in a 'struggle for survival' is applied rather unrestrainedly in Baden-Powell's writing at the service of an imperialism which Herbert Spencer himself would have rejected. Other nations that could formerly only look on and admire, it was claimed, were now directly competing with Britain in the race for colonies and commerce. If the British did not protect their gains, Baden-Powell admonished, then the same fate would befall them as the decadent Romans:

> And it will largely depend upon you, the younger generation of Britons that are now growing up to be the men of the Empire, [he urged] don't be disgraced like the young Romans who lost the Empire of their forefathers by being wishy-washy slackers without any go or patriotism in them. Play-up! Each man in his place, and play the game![38]

Another prerequisite for conservative philosophies of national revitalization before 1914 was a formula combining patriotism with social reform broadly known as social imperialism.[39] Its leading spokesmen were consulted by Baden-Powell during the promotional phase of his

Boy Scout scheme.[40] Sidney and Beatrice Webb used the argument
that the best hope of securing the Fabian social reforms which they
favoured lay in persuading the imperialists, particularly the Liberal
Imperialists, that the interests of a great Empire required the rearing
of an imperial race.[41] More overt social imperialists, such as Arthur
Pearson, Chairman of Joseph Chamberlain's Tariff Reform League
and proprietor of the *Daily Express*, wanted to achieve a blend of class
conciliation and social reform that would appease the discontented
working class. They were to find convenient allies in youth movements,
such as Scouting, which endorsed a common patriotism above class
distinctions:

> Remember, whether rich or poor, from castle or from slum, you are
> all Britons in the first place, and you've got to keep Britain up
> against outside enemies, [declaimed Baden-Powell] you have to
> stand shoulder to shoulder to do it. If you are divided among your-
> selves you are doing harm to your country. You must sink your
> differences.[42]

Imperialism, social Darwinism, the cult of national efficiency and certain
fashionable attitudes towards social reform are among the intellectual
currents which all found their way into the influential Scouting ideology
of the pre-1914 phase.[43] This is not to ignore other important ingredients, such as the romantic woodcraft naturalism of the American
youth leader, Ernest Thompson Seton,[44] or the public-school manliness ethos of Charterhouse. But the familiar *canard* that Scouting was
merely a game should not delude anyone into believing that Baden-
Powell was more concerned with the woodcraft means than the
patriotic end.[45] Scouting was viewed by the Chief Scout and his
most loyal supporters primarily as a form of moral and physical training to prevent national decadence. Like many other movements or
pressure groups, Scouting shared the tendency to start with a particular
aim and while pursuing it to expand its claims until it offered nothing
less than 'a revolution in national ideals.'[46] Baden-Powell promised to
restore much needed 'character' in the modern boy so as to prevent the
'sapping' of the nation's moral fibre which was, apparently, in danger of
imminent collapse.[47] A change in national attitudes was the essential
precondition for the acceptance of his remedy, which was in itself
designed to bring the change about.

But ideas alone cannot create a particular historical event. At the
more prosaic level of practical planning, Baden-Powell relied upon the

advice and assistance of two already well-established youth organizations to help him in the launching of his new movement. For without
the encouragement of William Smith, the founder of the Boys' Brigade,
he might never have converted *Aids to Scouting* into a format suitable
for application to boys.[48] And if it had not been for the YMCA, the
founder of Scouting would have been without a ready-made, nation-
wide platform to put his ideas into circulation.[49] After a certain preliminary sounding out of opinion, [50] the first experimental Boy Scout
camp was held on Brownsea Island in Poole Harbour, Dorset, from 29
July to 9 August 1907.[51] Above all, it was the brilliant publicity
campaign master-minded by Arthur Pearson and his publishing firm
that helped to create a favourable climate of opinion for Scouting.
'He was, I think, the first public man to whom I spoke of a Boy Scout
movement,' said Baden-Powell of his Maecenas, 'and his belief that
there was something in it encouraged me to go ahead with it.'[52] Just
before the camp deadline, Baden-Powell and Pearson had entered into
a preliminary agreement by which the publisher guaranteed to supply
financial backing of a thousand pounds, provide an office, and publish
The Scout, a weekly penny magazine. On his side, Baden-Powell committed himself to travelling around the country giving promotional lectures
while, with the assistance of one of Pearson's editors, preparing the
remaining parts of *Scouting for Boys* for publication.[53] The famous
newspaper publisher was not simply making a philanthropic gesture,
for he saw both the commercial and social-imperialist potential of a
scheme whose intrinsic aim was to improve the physical and moral
standard of British boyhood.

Owing to the association with Pearson, 'there was a prevalent feeling . . . that the scheme was being run as a money-making venture.'[54]
Certainly the business side of the successful promotion of Scouting has
seldom received its due attention. Perhaps it is felt that to describe in
detail the selling of an idea commercially is to downgrade the alleged
'spontaneity' of its appeal.[55] For instance, in order to secure a larger
sale, the book that was to bring into being the new youth movement,
Scouting for Boys, came out in six fortnightly parts at fourpence a
copy before being issued in hard covers.[56]

If we are to make a success of the scheme, [wrote Baden-Powell
with public relations acumen] we want the first part of the book
published as soon as possible in order to catch the public when they
are still hot and keen from my lectures.[57]

In any case, the impact of the Scout handbook was far-reaching, probably achieving as much as any other contemporary work in transforming the attitudes of adult youth workers towards the training of the young. Sub-titled *A handbook for instruction in good citizenship through woodcraft*, *Scouting for Boys* was divided into ten chapters, and further sub-divided into twenty eight 'camp-fire yarns', on topics such as scoutcraft, campaigning, camp life, tracking, woodcraft, endurance, chivalry, life-saving and patriotism. In a readable, pithy style, pitched at an easily understood level, what on the surface appeared a hotchpotch of unrelated topics interspersed with anecdotes and bits of instruction was in actuality a skilled blend of practical information, political treatise and woodcraft training. No wonder it has been compared to a boy's version of the *Reader's Digest*.

Although the evidence suggests that, initially, Baden-Powell had not planned to start a separate organization,[58] he had over-estimated the ability of the already existing youth movements to adapt his Boy Scout scheme to their own programmes.[59] All over England, boys collected the fortnightly parts of *Scouting for Boys* as they appeared on the bookstalls, formed troops unaided and then persuaded favoured adults to become their Scoutmasters.[60] Thus some kind of supervision or control of self-proclaimed Boy Scout troops and self-appointed Scoutmasters became urgent. This led to the setting up of local advisory committees, the appointment of travelling inspectors and the instalment of a Managing Secretary in the new Boy Scout Headquarters at Westminster.[61] The next stage in the rapid growth of the movement was to define organizational structures laid down in the various circulars, amalgamating all local committees into county committees to be called Scout Councils.[62] The difficulty of ensuring genuine local autonomy while maintaining a uniform national policy was never really resolved. Expansion meant the growth of bureaucratic centralization whatever Baden-Powell's own feelings about 'the infernal creeping in everywhere of formality and red tape.'[63]

Scouting was run on what appeared to be democratic lines, with a chain of command reaching down from the Chief Scout to the Governing Council's Executive Committee, from County Scout Councils to local District Scout Councils, and to local committees with some representation of the ordinary Scoutmaster. Yet since none of this 'democratic' machinery was open to election, there was no means by which the rank-and-file could influence the policy or change the leadership of the movement. Even the local Scout Commissioner was, in general, appointed without reference to Scoutmasters in the area.[64] 'Theoret-

ically, the movement is patriarchal in its forms of government,' wrote
one acute internal critic in 1918, 'practically, it is a compromise between
democracy and bureaucracy with a decided bias towards autocracy.'[65]
Partly this was an outcome of the high-handed, often insensitive,
behaviour of the Headquarters staff, and partly a result of Baden-
Powell's own feeling, as the founder of Scouting, that the time was not
yet ripe for having men elected to the Scout Council 'who might not
want to see the Movement developed in the way he wished.'[66] The
only real threats to this system of management came from the querul-
ous London Scout District: in 1909 led by the briefly appointed London Scout Commissioner, Sir Francis Vane, and in 1920 by John Hargrave, Headquarters' Commissioner for Camping and Woodcraft. Both
were compelled to resign from Scouting after attacking what they
interpreted as its militarist and imperialist tendencies.[67] As J. A. Kyle,
the disputatious Headquarters Managing Secretary, put it with some
understatement, London 'was always an unquiet area and a bit of a
nuisance.'[68]

The outbreak of the First World War introduced that inevitable
trial of patriotism, character and national survival for which Baden-
Powell had prepared the Boy Scout organization. It offered an opportunity to show their invaluable dependability as a national auxiliary. For
a very important motive in the initial formation of the Scout movement was to assist in the defence and effective maintenance of the
British Empire. Scouting made its own contribution towards creating
that mood of sustained patriotism among the young that led to mass
volunteering on the outbreak of war. 'Feelings of extreme patriotism
stifled all my ideals of international fellowship,' wrote one Boy Scout
in retrospect, 'I confess that I thought only of my country at this
time.'[69] Boy Scouts found themselves giving air-raid warnings, helping
with the flax harvest, acting as messengers, guarding reservoirs, running
mobile canteens in munitions factories and performing numerous other
duties on the Home Front.[70] They also looked out for men at country
railway stations whose resolution to enlist might falter if they lost
their way to the recruiting station: 'the timely arrival of the Scout
would often turn the scales in favour of the Country when a man was
wavering.'[71] The 1st Enfield (St James') Troop, in camp at Beachy
Head when war was declared, were soon checking up on spies along
the coastal road, 'and in fact reported to the Police the whereabouts of
two well-dressed gentlemen, speaking good English, but with a distinct
guttural accent.'[72] Their domestic mobilization as a part of the general
war effort won the Boy Scouts an entire chapter in *The Times History*

of the War.[73] A lesser-known contribution of Scouting to national defence was the formation by Baden-Powell of the Scouts Defence Corps. Its object was to 'form a trained force of young men who would be immediately available for the defence of the country should their services be required during the war.'[74]

The post-war period witnessed a subtle and effective re-orientation of Scouting which placed the emphasis firmly on class harmony, national unity and peaceful reconstruction,[75] aligning the movement solidly behind middle-of-the-road public opinion. Strenuous tours,[76] and the strains of overwork and age, meant that Baden-Powell increasingly left the day-to-day direction of the movement to his Headquarters Commissioners; though they were constantly deluged with his suggestions and proposals for development. During this period of seeming liberalization, Scouting projected an image of League of Nations internationalism and later of world Commonwealth brotherhood, rather than of the militarism and imperialism which the British Left persisted in identifying with the figure-head of Baden-Powell.[77] Thus in 1923, when the Chief Scout attempted to get the Labour Party more fully represented on the General Council of the Scout Association, both Ramsay MacDonald and George Lansbury turned him down for political reasons.[78] But whereas in 1908, Baden-Powell had denounced trade-unionists as 'paid professional agitators' and 'enemies of our country', in the 1920s he recognized that the unions 'have grown up to be great organizations for safeguarding the workers.'[79] Labour was now portrayed as a National Institution which believed in Education for Citizenship.

One interesting feature of Scout expansion was the development of the Rover sections which were established in 1919, although they were never more than a small minority of the entire movement. Despite the derisive critical onslaughts in recent years on Baden-Powell's unfortunate *Rovering to Success* (1922), the Rovers usefully extended Scouting to the over-fourteen age group and by 1928 they were providing 30 per cent of new Scoutmasters.[80] Throughout the 1920s, Scouting retained its overwhelming position as a mass youth movement, increasing its total numbers in Britain alone from 232,000 in 1920 to 422,000 in 1930.[81] During the early 1930s, however, there is evidence of a decline in impetus, particularly in those areas worst hit by the industrial depression, which was also experienced by most other British youth movements — with the partial exception of the Boys' Brigade. To some extent, this can be accounted for by the proliferation of new leisure activities, marked by the advent of hiking and the dramatic growth of the Youth Hostels Association.[82] As Baden-Powell's health deteriorated — he underwent a serious operation in 1934 — the absence of his charismatic presence was another contributory factor moderating the movement's rate of expansion. Compelled to retire from active leadership in 1937, as he announced at the Dutch World Jamboree, Baden-Powell spent his last years in Kenya where he died in 1941. In the 1930s, it was the well-publicized International Scout Conferences and Jamborees which did most to consolidate the predominance of Scouting as a world-wide youth movement.[83] At home, juvenile unemployment, the increasing strains on Baden-Powell's leadership, and the financial effects of the economic recession on the movement, all combined to slow down Scouting recruitment until the Second World War.

Yet in the decade from 1908 to 1919, no other influence upon British boyhood came anywhere near Baden-Powell's movement. Some, however, like novelist Evelyn Waugh, felt that 'the Scouts fell far short of the expectations raised by the books of Baden-Powell.'[84] The actual timing of the appearance of the first Boy Scout may be explained as an outcome of the post-Boer War mood of imperial decline and social reassessment. In discussing the general origins of the movement, however, the historian needs to go back further, at least to Thomas Hughes's idealization of Rugby and the 'muscular Christianity' of the third quarter of the nineteenth century. Despite subsequent new directions,[85] the ideological roots of Scouting remain buried in the public-school ethos of Charterhouse in the 1870s, the methods of colonial warfare in the 1880s and 1890s, and the intellectual climate of the 1900s. While the Boys' Brigade originated, to a great extent, in the social dilemmas of Glasgow during the early 1880s, the Boy Scouts could only have emerged against the real and imagined dangers of pre-1914 England. Scouting is one expression of a general cultural movement at the turn of the century among the European middle classes, reflecting the fears, aspirations and self-doubts of an Edwardian military caste anxious to preserve its prestige in a world disturbed by class conflict, international crisis and the threat of national decline.[86]

Notes

1.   E. K. Wade, *The Piper of Pax* (London, 1931 edn.), Foreword, p. 11. Baden-Powell (1857-1941). See Biographical Notes.

2.   Her sons were Sir George Smyth Baden-Powell (1847-1898), Conservative M.P. for Kirkdale, Liverpool (1885-1898); Henry Baden (1841-1901),

step-son, Judge of the Chief Court, Lahore; Henry Warington Smyth (1847-1921), Admiralty Barrister, King's Counsel; Frank Smyth (1850-1933), barrister and artist/sculptor; and Baden Fletcher Smyth, an aviation pioneer and President of the Aeronautic Society. All the children were christened Smyth, but not Baden.

3. Under the will of Thomas Sutton, the founder of Charterhouse, a free education was provided for forty 'Gownboys' in the form of a scholarship originally meant for poor boys. By 1870, 'reform' of the public schools allowed Baden-Powell's family to obtain a nomination from the Duke of Marlborough, who had recently been made a School Governor.

4. The Revd Canon Dr William Haig-Brown (1823-1907). See Biographical Notes.

5. See William Hillcourt with Olave, Lady Baden-Powell, *Baden-Powell: the two lives of a hero* (London, 1964), p. 22.

6. The self-reliance inculcated by the Scout movement has been so much stressed that it is salutary to point out that it has been seen by one observer as demanding conformity to a code of behaviour as strict as that of any public school. See W. S. Adams, *Edwardian Portraits* (London, 1957), p. 131.

7. Baden-Powell, 'The Boy Scouts in connection with National Training and National Service', *Royal United Services Institute Journal*, Vol. LV (Jan.-June, 1911), p. 581. This was a lecture given to the Institute on 29 March 1911 with R. B. Haldane in the Chair.

8. Anon., *Scout Association Annual Report and Yearbook, 1919*, p. 6. The long term effects of this 'public school spirit' on the character moulding of the English ruling classes have recently been called into question. See Corelli Barnett, *The Collapse of British Power* (London, 1971), p. 37.

9. Edward C. Mack, *Public Schools and British Opinion* (London, 1938), pp. 80-81.

10. See David Newsome, *Godliness and Good Learning* (London, 1961), chap 4. 'Race suicide is possible . . . it may be brought about by popular tendencies towards effeminacy and self-indulgence, with the consequent result of the relaxation of the moral and physical fibre.' Cf. Anon., 'Sport and Decadence', *The Quarterly Review*, Vol. CCXII, No. 421 (Oct., 1909), p. 487.

11. Baden-Powell, *R.U.S.I. Journal*, p. 586.

12. Cited on the dust jacket of E. E. Reynolds, *Baden-Powell* (London, 1942); taken from a review of the first impression by the *Catholic Herald*.

13. Byron Farewell, *Queen Victoria's Little Wars* (London, 1973), p. 351.

14. Baden-Powell, *Scouting for Boys* (London, 1909 edn.), p. 301. This reaction to barracks-square drill was confirmed by his experience of the Boer War, where 'men who had never had a day's drill in their lives' were still 'effective in the field against our trained troops through their individual intelligence, pluck, and the will to succeed.' Cited in Hillcourt, p. 288.

15. Donald Baden-Powell to the BBC Talks Department, February 1957. Collection of Francis Baden-Powell. Aged only nine, Donald was a rather unwilling participant in the 1907 Brownsea Island Scout Camp.

16. Cited in E. E. Reynolds, p. 74.

17. Cf. *Vedette* (London, 1883); *Reconnaissance and Scouting* (London, 1884); *Cavalry Instruction* (London, 1885); *Pig-sticking or Hog-hunting* (London, 1889); *The Downfall of Prempeh* (London, 1896); *The Matabele Campaign* (London, 1897); *Aids to Scouting for N.C.O.s and Men* (London, 1899).

18. See Brian Gardner, *Mafeking: A Victorian Legend* (London, 1966), pp. 35-37; Rhodesia and Bechuanaland Protectorate, *Standing Orders for Colonel Baden-Powell's Frontier Force* (Cape Town, 1899), Section XII;

Baden-Powell to Lord Wolseley, 1 July 1900, Wolseley Papers, Hove
Library, Sussex; Hillcourt, p. 162; E. E. Reynolds, chap. 8.

19.   See Baden-Powell, typewritten Ms., 'The Origins of "Scouting for Boys"',
(n.d.), Scout Archives, London; E. E. Reynolds, chap. 7. From 1900 to
1901, the enterprising editor of *Boys of the Empire* serialized some of the
contents of *Aids to Scouting* under the heading of 'The Boy Scout', which
was the first known use of the term.

20.   Winston Churchill, *Great Contemporaries* (London, 1959 edn.), p. 298.
But writing to his sister-in-law, Baden-Powell claimed that 'the new appoint-
ment is the top of the tree for a cavalry man and of course I am very, very
pleased and a great deal astonished at having been selected for it.' Baden-
Powell to Frances Baden-Powell, 14 June 1903; collection of Francis
Baden-Powell.

21.   See Hillcourt, pp. 275-276.

22.   But in 1920 he wrote to Winston Churchill: 'You will find that the Scouts
are likely to provide a fairly hearty contribution of men to the Territorials
in the next few years . . . and with the Scout movement developing as it
now is I see a big possibility that way.' Baden-Powell to Churchill, holograph
draft, 10 May 1920, Scout Archives, Vol. IV, Ref. 9.

23.   Anon., ('M.W.'), 'A Point of View on Scouting' in *Home Words*, Vol. XLI,
No. 1 (Jan., 1911), p. 24.

24.   Baden-Powell to Town Clerks and YMCA Secretaries, 28 October 1907,
reprinted in Paul C. Richards (ed.), *The Founding of the Boy Scouts as
seen through the letters of Lord Baden-Powell, 1907-1908* (Massachusetts,
1973), doc. 3.

25.   Cited in W. S. Adams, p. 123.

26.   Viz., *Report of Committee on War Office Organization*, Cd. 580, 1901;
*Report of Royal Commission on the Care and Treatment of the Sick and
Wounded during the South African Campaign*, Cd. 453, 1901; *Report of
the Elgin Commission of Inquiry into the South African War*, Cd. 1789,
1903; *Report of the Butler Committee into the Disposal of War Stores*,
Cd. 2435, 1905.

27.   Baden-Powell, *Scouting for Boys* (London, 1908 edn.), p. 208.

28.   See *Report of the Physical Deterioration Committee*, Cd. 2210, 1904;
Samuel Hynes, *The Edwardian Turn of Mind* (London, 1968), pp. 23-24;
Maurice Bruce, *The Coming of the Welfare State* (London, 1961), p. 192.

29.   Baden-Powell, *R.U.S.I. Journal*, p. 595.

30.   Baden-Powell, 'Deposition as to Origins of Scout Movement', affidavit of
24 May 1918: when the Chief Scout appeared at the American Consulate
General in Cavendish Square, London, as a witness in the case of Boy
Scouts of America vs. American Boy Scouts, before Supreme Court of New
York County. Scout Archives, London.

31.   E.g., Baden-Powell often quoted the words of George Wyndham, Tory
Imperialist MP and Tariff Reformer, that 'the same causes which brought
about the downfall of the Great Roman Empire are working today in
Great Britain.' See Baden-Powell, *Scouting for Boys* (London, 1908 edn.),
p. 335. Another influence was: Anon. (Elliot E. Mills), *The Decline and
Fall of the British Empire* (Oxford, 1905): — a political satire written by
a young Tory National Service League supporter.

32.   See Geoffrey Searle, *The Quest for National Efficiency: a study in British
politics and political thought, 1899-1914* (Oxford, 1971); E. J. T. Brennan,
*Education for National Efficiency: the contribution of Sidney and Beatrice
Webb* (London, 1975).

33.   See Baden-Powell, *Today and Tomorrow*, (n.d. 1916?), p. 4, for a chart of

'national inefficiencies, their causes and remedies.' British Library of Political and Economic Science; Searle, p. 66.

34. H. G. Wells, *The New Machiavelli* (Penguin edn., 1966), p. 254. This sentence occurs in a paragraph expressing admiration for the ideas of 'Imperial patriotism' and 'social efficiency'. The hero of the novel eventually espouses the Ideal Efficiency of the Great State.

35. See Gertrude Himmelfarb, 'Varieties of Social Darwinism' in *Victorian Minds* (London, 1968), chap. 7; Raymond Williams, 'Social Darwinism' in *The Listener*, 23 November 1972, pp. 696-700; H. W. Koch, 'Social Darwinism as a factor in the "New Imperialism" ', in H. W. Koch (ed.), *The Origins of the First World War* (London, 1972), pp. 329-354.

36. See John Gillis, *Youth and History: tradition and change in European age relations, 1770-present* (London, 1974), p. 144.

37. T. H. Manners-Howe, 'Church Lads' Brigade: work which the nation ought to do' in the *Graphic*, 6 August 1910, p. 222.

38. Baden-Powell, *Scouting for Boys* (London, 1909 edn.), p. 267.

39. See Bernard Semmel, *Imperialism and Social Reform: English social imperial thought, 1895-1914* (London, 1960), chap. 1; Robert J. Scally, *The Origins of the Lloyd George Coalition: the politics of social imperialism, 1900-1918* (London, 1975).

40. Partisans of Joseph Chamberlain's social imperialist programme, such as Lord Roberts, Kitchener, Lord Charles Beresford, the 12th Earl of Meath and Sir Arthur Pearson, received copies of two four-page circulars sent out by Baden-Powell, *Boy Scouts, A Suggestion* and *Boy Scouts, Summary of a Scheme*, both printed in 1907 and given in full in E. E. Reynolds, *The Scout Movement* (London, 1950), pp. 9-13.

41. See Royden Harrison, 'Wonders of the Webbs', review of E. J. T. Brennan, op. cit., in *New Society*, Vol. XXX, No. 669, 31 July 1975, p. 261; Bernard Semmel, chap. 4.

42. Baden-Powell, *Scouting for Boys* (London, 1909 edn.), p. 270.

43. See Paul Wilkinson, 'English Youth Movements, 1908-1930' in *The Journal of Contemporary History*, Vol. IV, No. 2 (April, 1969), p. 12.

44. See Brian Morris, 'Ernest Thompson Seton and the origins of the Woodcraft Movement' in *The Journal of Contemporary History*, Vol. V, No. 2 (1970), pp. 183-194; Heinz Reichling, *Ernest Thompson Seton und die Woodcraft Bewegung in England* (Bonn, 1937), chap. 2. In July 1906, Baden-Powell received a copy of Seton's *The Birch-bark Roll of the Woodcraft Indians* (1906), and, according to his diary, met the author a few months later in London.

45. See William Mc. G. Eager, *Making Men: a history of boys' clubs and related movements in Great Britain* (London, 1953), pp. 334-335.

46. See *Home Words*. In 1911 Sir Trevor Dawson, a managing director of Vickers Ltd., accused Baden-Powell of over-stating his case by making 'sweeping assertions'. See Scout Archives, Vol. II, 1910-1913, Ref. 68.

47. See early Scout publications and the journalism of Baden-Powell, 1908-1911: Vols. I-II Scout Archives; Baden-Powell's Miscellaneous Writings, 1914-1919: Vols. XXIII-XXIV, Lord Robert Baden-Powell, Ripley, Surrey.

48. In May 1903, Baden-Powell had taken the Chair at the annual Albert Hall demonstration of the Boys' Brigade. In April 1904 he acted as Inspecting Officer of the Annual Drill Inspection and Review in Glasgow, where William Smith suggested that he re-write *Aids to Scouting* in a form that could be applied to the training of boys. In June 1906 the *Boys' Brigade Gazette* carried the first preliminary proposals for the organization of Boy Scouts.

49. From October 1907 to February 1908, Baden-Powell gave lectures on Scouting which introduced it to 'the British public in the most effective possible way.' See Sir Percy Everett, *The First Ten Years* (Ipswich, 1948), p. 20. The majority of these lectures were sponsored by local YMCAs, held in their halls, and advertised by Henry Shaw, working from Arthur Pearson's offices. See E. E. Reynolds, *Baden-Powell*, pp. 147-148.

50. Even before Brownsea Island, Baden-Powell had already circularized the *Boys' Brigade Gazette* programme suggestions to men like Lord Roberts. A more comprehensive draft, 'Boy Patrols', of February 1907, became incorporated into *Boy Scouts, A Suggestion,* of November 1907, the first official printed circular.

51. This historic island site belonged to a Mr. Charles Van Raalte, whom Baden-Powell had met while on a fishing holiday in Ireland. Twenty boys were present in four patrols, drawn from sons of the General's friends or from the Boys' Brigade in Poole and Bournemouth. They camped under canvas on the south shore of the island. See Baden-Powell, Circular III, *Boy Scouts, A Successful Trial,* Nov., 1907, Scout Archives, Vol. III, Ref. 3; Hillcourt, chap. 17; Percy Everett, chap. 2; E. E. Reynolds, chap. 11.

52. Cited in Sydney Dark, *The Life of Sir Arthur Pearson* (London, 1922), p. 84.

53. See Hillcourt, p. 263; Paul C. Richards (ed.), *passim;* Percy Everett, chap. 3.

54. J. A. Kyle, 'The Early Days of the Boy Scout Movement from Within' in *The Trail,* Vol. V, No. 48 (Jan., 1922), p. 16.

55. The fullest account of the negotiations with Pearson's and the contractual wrangling over publication rights and royalties is given in Hillcourt, chaps. 16-18. Eventually Pearson's were given a five year contract: for publishing *The Scout* and using Baden-Powell's weekly feature, the company was to pay £500 cash and 10 per cent of the profits of the paper; for publishing *Scouting for Boys,* Pearson's would pay a straight 20 per cent royalty which went into the Boy Scout Treasury.

56. The first part of *Scouting for Boys* appeared on the bookstalls on 15/16 January 1908. Cloth bound, at two shillings a copy, it was published by Horace Cox, who did most of Pearson's printing, on 1 May 1908. The fortnightly parts were reprinted four times during 1908, five times in volume form. Later, Pearson's issued their own cheap cloth-bound edition at one shilling, which sold over 5,000 copies a month. Indeed, *Scouting for Boys,* translated into many languages, may rank third after the Bible and Shakespeare among the world's best-sellers.

57. Baden-Powell to Peter Keary, 24 November 1907. Cited Paul C. Richards (ed.), doc. 5, n.p. Keary was Pearson's Managing Director handling commercial agreements and contractual negotiations with Baden-Powell.

58. In a memo of October 1908, Baden-Powell wrote that Scouting 'was started with the idea that its chief points might form useful additions to the present attractions or training held out to boys by the different organizations.' Cited in Eileen K. Wade, *Twenty One Years of Scouting* (London, 1929), p. 78.

59. The Boys' Brigade and the Church Lads' Brigade both made half-hearted attempts to establish scouting branches within their own organizations but neither met with much success. More prominent by far were the Life Saving Scouts and Guides of the Salvation Army, founded by Colonel Sladen in 1914, specializing in First Aid, and by 1930 the second largest woodcraft movement. In 1948 they finally gave up their separate existence and joined mainstream Scouting as Salvation Army Scouts. See P. B. Nevill, *My Scouting Story* (London, 1960), p. 180.

60. E.g., in London, having run themselves for several months without adult supervision, a Scoutmaster was not introduced into the 5th Islington Troop until it was already 25 strong. The 2nd Islington ran their own club as the 'Scouting Boys' for about two months before their Sunday School teacher consented to become Scoutmaster. See Anon., 'The Islington Scout Groups: a brief historical survey' in *The Islington Boy Scouts Fortieth Anniversary Handbook, 1908-1948* (Islington, 1948), pp. 60-73.

61. Cf. Typescript circular, 'The Development of the Organization of Scouting for Boys', 28 September 1908, Scout Archives, Vol. 1, Ref. 50; Hillcourt, p. 290.

62. Cf. Circular '0', 'The Boy Scouts Organization', 24 June 1909, Scout Archives, Vol. 1, Ref. 51. On the introduction of the patrol and badge systems see E. E. Reynolds, *Scout Movement*, chaps. 6-8.

63. Scoutmaster Dr T. S. Lukis, a Toynbee Hall Resident, objected to the commercial management techniques of Arthur Pearson and blamed excessive red-tape for alienating the Boys' Brigade and undermining the power of the local Scoutmaster. See T. S. Lukis, 'The Boy Scout Movement' in *The Toynbee Record*, Vol. XXI, No. 7 (April, 1909), pp. 125-128.

64. See 'Scout Notes and News: A Scoutmaster's Complaint' in the *Daily Sketch*, 13 July 1912; Sir Francis Vane, 'A Danger in the Boy Scout Movement' in the *Westminster Gazette*, 1 March 1910; E. E. Reynolds, p. 77.

65. 'Hawkeye' (pseudon.), 'Growth and Organization of the Boy Scout Movement' in *The Trail*, Vol. 1, No. 1 (Feb., 1918), p. 5.

66. P. B. Nevill, p. 82.

67. See J. O. Springhall, 'The Boy Scouts, Class and Militarism in relation to British Youth Movements, 1908-1930' in *International Review of Social History*, Vol. XVI, Pt. 2 (1971), Section IV, pp. 148-155. Vane went on to take over the Presidency of the pacifist British Boy Scouts, later the Sabbatarian-led Brotherhood of British Boy Scouts, and Hargrave became the Head Man of the Kibbo Kift Kindred, a woodcraft movement, in the 1920s (cf. chap. 7).

68. J. A. Kyle, *The Trail*, No. 49 (Feb., 1922), p. 43.

69. F. Haydn Dimmock, *Bare Knee Days* (London, 1937), pp. 43-44. After the war, Dimmock became editor of *The Scout*.

70. See reports on Boy Scouts' war service in Scout Archives, Vols. III and IIIa; E. E. Reynolds, *Baden-Powell*, chap. 14; Baden-Powell, *Guarding the Coasts of Britain: what the Sea Scouts are doing* (London, 1918).

71. Anon., *The Boy Scouts and the Great War: how the Boy Scouts have helped the home-land in the hours of peril* (London, 1915), p. 12.

72. Anon., 'Past and Present: a review of the Enfield Scout Groups' in *Enfield Boy Scouts, 1957 Jubilee Year Book* (Enfield, 1957), p. 21.

73. Anon., *The Times History of the War*, Vol. XVII (London, 1919), chap. 253.

74. Baden-Powell, *Markmanship for Boys: The Red Feather and how to win it* (London, 1915), p. 62. The 'red feather' was awarded to Boy Scouts who passed recruiting tests for the Corps, including rifle-shooting and military drill.

75. See Baden-Powell, *Scouting Towards Reconstruction* (London, 1918), p. 12; Paul Wilkinson, 'A Study of English Uniformed Youth Movements, 1883-1935', M.A. thesis, 1968, University of Wales, p. 116.

76. 'My wife and I are having a most enjoyable and successful tour — though strenuous,' Baden-Powell wrote to Lord Selbourne of his 1927 South African tour, 'for me a bit too strenuous at times, and I have been knocked up on two or three occasions in consequence.' Baden-Powell to Selbourne,

19 February 1927, Ms. Selbourne 72, Fols. 186, Bodleian Library, Oxford. Baden-Powell was aged 70 in 1927.

77.   See Leslie Paul, *The Republic of Children* (London, 1938), p. 23; I. O. Evans, *Woodcraft and World Service* (London, 1930), p. 32; Leslie Paul, *Courage has a New Face* (2nd edn. 1930), leaflet, n.p., speech to the Woodcraft Althing; copy of Young Communist League Circular, 19 October 1927, Scout Archives, Vol. VI, Ref. 56.

78.   See E. E. Reynolds, *Baden-Powell*, pp. 215-216, for the text of their refusals. Ramsay MacDonald could not do anything which would 'raise controversy on non-essentials inside the [Labour] Party.' MacDonald to Baden-Powell, 1 February 1923, Scout Archives, Vol. IV, Ref. 97.

79.   Baden-Powell, *Scouting for Boys* (London, 1908 edn.), p. 337; Baden-Powell, *Rovering to Success: a book of life-sport for young men* (London, 1922), p. 142.

80.   See Norman Mackenzie, 'Sweating it out with B-P' in the *New Statesman*, 15 October 1965, p. 555, for criticism of *Rovering to Success;* Paul Wilkinson, 1968 M.A. thesis, p. 125, for a reply; on the Rovers cf. P. B. Nevill, chaps. 4-5.

81.   See Appendix II, 'U.K. Scout Membership by Sections, 1912-1941.'

82.   Whereas the 1931 Youth Hostel Association Handbook claimed only 16,000 members, throughout the 1930s membership rose at a rate of approximately 10,000 every year, and by 1939 reached 83,417. See Oliver Coburn, *Youth Hostel Story* (London, 1950); Wilkinson, pp. 204-209.

83.   International Scout Conferences met every other year, served by an International Committee and a Bureau based in London. Up until the Second World War, World Jamborees had been held at: Olympia, London (1920); Copenhagen, Denmark (1924); Arrowe Park, Birkenhead (1929); Godollo, Hungary (1933); and Vogelenzang, Holland (1937). In 1924 it was still thought worthwhile to organize a separate Imperial Jamboree at Wembley Stadium for Dominion and Colonial Scouts.

84.   Evelyn Waugh, *A Little Learning, the first volume of an autobiography* (London, 1973 edn.), p. 89. Waugh belonged to a school patrol in one of the local Hampstead troops during the First World War. Another well-known Boy Scout was ex-Prime Minister Harold Wilson, Patrol Leader in the Milnsbridge Baptist Scouts, Huddersfield.

85.   See Scout Association, *The Chief Scout's Advance Party Report*, 1966, which recommended the adoption of a new long-trousered uniform, changes in the Scout Law and Promise and the substitution of Cub Scouts and Venture Scouts for the old-style Wolf Cubs and Rovers. Cf. Robin Mead, 'Scouting Prepares for the Future', *The Times*, 10 July 1971. A traditionalist break-away movement called the Baden-Powell Boy Scouts has been set up since 1971 to re-instate 'the basic ideals and discipline' of old-fashioned, outdoor Scouting. Cf. Scout Action Group, *A Boy Scout Black Paper* (London, 1970).

86.   See John Gillis, *Youth and History*, p. 141; M. S. Anderson, *The Ascendancy of Europe: aspects of European history, 1815-1914* (London, 1972), pp. 300-311; Gerhard Masur, *Prophets of Yesterday: Studies in European Culture, 1890-1914* (Yale, 1961), chap. 8.

4 DUTY AND DISCIPLINE

Before the mid-1880s, the history of the cadet movement in Britain,
with some few exceptions, was predominantly that of middle-class
public or private school units attached to their local Volunteers. After
1911, thanks to R. B. Haldane at the War Office, cadets were to become
an integral part of the State's military apparatus, supplying potential
recruits for the Territorials. But between 1885 and 1910, non-school
cadets offer the significant historical paradigm of a voluntary youth
movement with a military foundation deliberately making an appeal,
almost as a form of social redemption, to working-class boys in large
cities. The nucleus of the first voluntary working-class cadet battalion
in London and forerunner of the British Army Cadet Force,[1] was in
the Southwark Cadet Corps. It will be considered here in some detail
because of Southwark's contribution to a more extensive scheme of
'scientific charity' for the moral regeneration of the London working
classes: which finds its fullest expression in the work of the Charity
Organization Society, a body that was 'professionally pioneering but
ideologically reactionary.'[2] And it is only by placing these working-
class cadet companies within the context of the 'settlement movement'
and their related network of boys' clubs, that a clear picture emerges
of their role in the social training of non-public-school youth.

Apart from some earlier, marginal manifestations, cadets first appear
in Britain, cointerminous with the revival of the Volunteer movement;
at the time of the military 'panic' of 1859 to 1860 over Napoleon III's
French invasion threat. Very few records of non-school or 'open'
cadet corps survive for this period, although doubtless some few existed
in a disorganized form. So it is safe to assume that, initially at least,
cadets were largely restricted to Volunteer corps of senior boys and
masters at the major English public schools, or were designed to act as
parental feeders for local Rifle Volunteer battalions.[3] These cadet
units arose semi-spontaneously at a time of imaginary national crisis,
for it was not until 1863 that the War Office formally authorized the
formation of cadet units as part of the Volunteers Act.[4] Following
this official encouragement, in the 1870s other English public schools,
such as Charterhouse and Dulwich College, started their own cadet or
rifle corps — one such cadet being the schoolboy Robert Baden-Powell.
Predictably, until 1886, when authority was given for raising cadet

battalions independently of Volunteer units, the strength of school cadet corps tended to wax and wane with the fortunes or misfortunes of their parent Volunteer battalions.[5] The results of this early period of cadet history were, therefore, spasmodic and largely confined to middle-class boys recruited from the major public schools. Until the outbreak of the Boer War led to an outburst of patriotic emotion, they were not regarded with a great deal of enthusiasm either by masters or boys.[6]

Taking advantage of the new regulations, the first attempt to use the idea of cadet training other than as a form of pre-service preparation for the Volunteers came in 1886 with the setting up of the East London Cadet Corps. It was to be found at the liberal — yet unorthodox — Toynbee Hall University Settlement in Whitechapel: a monument to Edward Denison and Arnold Toynbee, which ostensibly expressed the spirit of Balliol College, Oxford, rather than that of militarism.[7] The original inspiration for bringing working-class boys within the general ambience of the social values fostered by the public schools came from a Toynbee Hall Resident: the peripatetic Sir Francis Fletcher Vane who was to prove a thorn in the side for Baden-Powell when, in 1909, he briefly became London's first Boy Scout Commissioner.[8] 'Healthy physical exercise will make up for narrow surroundings; discipline will cultivate the virtues of obedience and self-control as well as reverence for law and order,' Sir Francis claimed for the cadets, and 'through *esprit de corps*, patriotism will grow; true patriotism will lead to a just appreciation of the duties of citizenship, and the part which the Anglo-Saxon race is called upon to play in the cause of progress.'[9]

Together with Canon Barnett, the rotund and balding first Warden of Toynbee Hall, Sir Francis visited the Whittington Boys' Club,[10] opened by Toynbee in 1885, to make an appeal for recruits. The resulting cadet corps was attached to the Tower Hamlets Rifle Volunteers, an efficient drill sergeant from the Tower of London was engaged and the quad of Toynbee Hall became a barrack-square — much to the annoyance of some of the more pacifically inclined Residents.[11] Not long after, when Vane left Toynbee Hall to join a trading syndicate promoted by W. T. Stead, Henry Nevinson — later to become one of England's most respected war correspondents — took over the running of the Corps, 'in the hopes of ensuring some small amount of benefit to the enfeebled and undersized youth of Whitechapel and Shadwell.'[12] Until 1887, Nevinson was assisted in this self-imposed task by another Toynbee Hall Resident, William Ingham Brooke,[13] who, on leaving Toynbee, started up a boys' club in Southwark — an area of London

that was to make one of the most positive contributions to the evolving
history of the cadet movement.

Southwark is one of the oldest of London's boroughs, with a history
dating back to Roman and Saxon times, when it was the greatest
traffic and trading centre in England.[14] Tied closely to the City of London, until the creation in 1900 of the Metropolitan Boroughs of Southwark and Bermondsey, it relied heavily on the stage-coach trade for the
success of its innumerable inns. The second half of the eighteenth
century saw a changing occupational pattern, however, with the building
of the great docks of Bermondsey and Rotherhithe. During the nineteenth century, urbanization accelerated, the docks were gradually
extended, canals built, roads improved and the stage-coach slowly gave
way to the railway. By the time Ingham Brooke moved there, Southwark
had in essence assumed its present form: railways had been built through
the borough, including the first 'electric tube railway' in London;
Tower Bridge had been built; there had been vast increases in housing
development; and the familiar wide streets leading to Blackfriars,
Southwark, London and Tower Bridges, had already reached complet-
ion.[15] Coincidental with Brooke's arrival, was the setting up of an early
experimental community centre in Southwark: the Red Cross Hall,
Cottages and Garden, which has been characterized as 'one of the
earliest and most attractive of humanity's counter-attacks on slumdom'.[16]
But the Red Cross centre can be viewed just as appropriately as representative of that attempt by the new urban squirearchy to restore the
whole traditional fabric of social control threatened by the metropolitan environment[17] – which also finds expression in the setting up of
the Southwark Cadet Corps.

The Red Cross Boys' Club, which Brooke started in Southwark, was
a portent of the rash of working boys' clubs that appeared all over
working-class areas of London in the last two decades of the nineteenth
century.[18] It also provides a direct link between the Charity Organization Society and the formation of the first London working-class cadet
battalion. For, as Secretary to the local COS branch, Brooke soon
came into contact with an early member working in the area as a rent
collector for the Church Commissioners: Octavia Hill, an energetic,
dumpy, spinster housing reformer and the woman chiefly responsible
for the building of the Red Cross complex, 'the good Squiress of the
great village.'[19] Enlisting her support, Brooke decided that the only
way to control the rowdy boys attending his boys' club was by repeating the experiment of the cadet corps which he had participated in while
at Toynbee Hall. Thinking that 'a little military discipline might teach

the boys how to behave,'[20] Octavia Hill warmly supported his plans for turning the club into a cadet corps.

Accordingly, Lord Wolseley was persuaded to preside over the inaugural meeting to launch the proposed Southwark Cadets, held on 30 May 1889 at the recently opened Red Cross Hall.[21] Its purpose was to set up 'a cadet corps of young lads living in Southwark like the one which has been so successful in Whitechapel.'[22] It was hoped to persuade local manufacturers, employers and City bankers to pay for uniforms and equipment, as it was intended to run the cadets on a completely self-assisted basis.[23] The first 25 recruits came, as might be expected, from the Red Cross Boys' Club and, after drilling them, Brooke proudly proclaimed to his benefactress, Octavia Hill, that 'military enthusiasm is the prevailing spirit in Red Cross Street.'[24] One of the first boys to get a uniform recalled much later: 'we drilled at the back of some model dwellings in White Cross Street and in the Red Cross Hall when it was wet and we learned the use of arms with old Snider Carbines.'[25] Uniform consisted of tunic, trousers, cap and belt with the later addition of great-coats, leggings and haversacks, indispensable for 'marching-out'.

> The effect of the discipline and *esprit de corps* on the lads is strongly marked; they are invariably quiet, steady and smart on parade, and their conduct leaves nothing to be desired, [wrote their Commanding Officer in his first report] considering some of the material on which these influences had to work the result is really surprising.[26]

Almost every cadet company in London was based on a working-boys' club, which in turn were associated with public-school missions or university settlements, whose youthful middle-class 'residents' regularly provided the officers.[27] In 1891 the Southwark Cadet Corps, absorbing the East London Cadet Corps started at Toynbee Hall, and the Eton College Mission Cadet Company, was transformed into the first 'battalion of boys of the labouring class' in London and it was the largest in Britain.[28] As the 1st London Cadet Battalion, the original nucleus of Southwark Cadets spread out their catchment area until, by the outbreak of the Boer War, they embraced large numbers of boys from Walworth, Lambeth, Blackfriars, Peckham and Kennington. A detailed narrative history of this Battalion could possibly be compiled from the scattered documentary sources that still survive,[29] but the emphasis would have to be on their attendance at public ceremonial functions, which gave them a 'corporate' participatory role in national life.[30] It is perhaps worth recording, nonetheless, that a great deal of the early success of the cadets in Southwark was due in no small measure to their drill instructor, Albert Salmond,[31] to the careful control over finances exercised by Octavia Hill and her co-Treasurer, Sydney Cockerell,[32] and to the services rendered to the Battalion over a period of 60 years by the indefatigable Lancelot Bennett.[33]

The social composition of the Southwark Cadet Corps is of interest both in its reflection of the juvenile employment structure of South London and for the insight it offers into the appeal such a youth movement exercised over working-class boys, 'whose view had hitherto been limited to their back-street, their board school, and workshop.'[34] For example, the enrolment book extant for 1889 to 1891, providing the occupations of nearly 500 boys, offers clear evidence of the large proportion of those enlisted in the cadets in Southwark who worked in the local printing or book-binding works.[35]

Table 1: Enrolment of Boys in Southwark Cadet Corps, 1889-1891[36]

Occupation	1889	1890	1891	Total	%
Skilled trades	65	96	32	193	39
Printing/book-binding	40*	71	29	140	28
Errand boys/messenger/ van boys	10	18	24	52	10
Warehouse/office boys	9	13	9	31	6
Apprentices	8	5	5	18	4
Clerical	1	9	5	15	3
Unclassified	22	20	6	48	10
Totals	155	232	110	497	100

* This figure includes 12 boys classified as 'printers' boy' which may refer either to a 'printers' devil' or an errand boy.

But as Lancelot Bennett, officer in command of 'B' Company of the Southwark Cadets, pointed out to the 1904 Physical Deterioration Committee, only a fraction of those boys initially employed in the printing trade would gain adult employment thereby, 'and it does not seem healthy or suitable for boys, particularly in the case of those who carry the damp paper about to the machines.'[37] Nearly two fifths of those enrolled from 1889 to 1891 (Table 1), are engaged in a variety of small crafts, working for brass-finishers, cabinet-makers, boiler-makers, glass-blowers and carpenters. Only 16 per cent are registered directly as errand boys or warehouse boys and so on, and they were shockingly prone to varicose veins from being constantly on their feet all day, running about performing errands.[38] A decade later, however, figures available for Southwark given by Bennett (Table 2), suggest that the number of cadets in skilled trades, which include printing, has declined while the ranks of the unskilled have swollen: testimony to the progressive casualization of the teenage labour market. This was an effect of the discontinuity between juvenile and adult employment which was an endemic feature of the occupational structure of late Victorian London.[39]

Table 2: Enrolment of Boys in Southwark Cadet Corps, 1899-1901[40]

Occupation	1899	1900	1901	Total	%
Skilled trades*	65	43	23	131	41
Errand boys/messenger/ van boys	21	23	21	65	20
Warehouse/office boys	30	28	21	79	24
Apprentices	7	-	3	10	3
Clerical	24	11	4	39	12
Totals	147	105	72	324	100

* Includes: 'printers' devils, machine minders and those learning a trade'. No separate statistics are provided for printing and book-binding.

According to returns made in 1899 by the Board of Trade to the House of Commons, of a representative sample of London school leavers, less than a third would take up apprenticeships leading to jobs classified as 'skilled', while 40 per cent would become errand or van boys.[41] This pattern of employment is reflected in Table 2, where the 144 boys registered as errand, messenger or warehouse boys and so on, now outnumber the 131 engaged in skilled trades, although the number of clerical workers has more than doubled between the two cadet enrolments surveyed. Thus in the 1890s, at least, there was a relatively greater — if inelastic — demand for unskilled teenage labour in London than for those in their twenties, even if, as has been suggested, it was

often an artificial result of the effort to reduce the competitive position
of adults.[42] Consequently, owing to the contraction of unskilled work
for young men of eighteen to twenty, the British Army — which drew
most of its recruits from the low-skilled[43] — gained a reputation as a
last resort for superannuated boy labour. Cadets entered the armed
forces, that is, as much as a result of the structure of juvenile employment in late-Victorian London as any other factor.[44] The problem
remains, however, why they chose this option rather than some other
alternative, such as emigration.

By the 1890s, cadet training was seen by its invariably public-school
officers as a method of preventing teenage 'lawlessness', while also
offering 'a counter attraction to the low Music Halls which are now so
much resorted to for want of more edifying relaxation.'[45] In 1905,
the Battalion's Commanding Officer, Colonel Beresford, opined that the
cadets provided 'for working class lads many of the advantages of that
Public School training which has so great an effect on moulding the
characters of the upper and middle classes.'[46] Cadet training was
justified as a method of mediating middle-class, public-school values: a
form of 'character' building that was strongly contrasted by its expo-
nents, such as Octavia Hill, with the 'ill educated, dirty, quarrelsome,
drunken, improvident, unrefined, possibly dishonest, possibly vicious'[47]
working-class society from which the cadets were recruited. Octavia
Hill's role in the setting up of the British cadet movement has so far
remained unacknowledged by the historian. It can be placed within the
same ideological framework of 'self-improvement' that motivated her
rigorous 'system' of housing management in Southwark. The stiff,
individualist sub-structure of her thought reflected the late-nineteenth-
century idea of 'scientific' charity, enshrined in the Charity Organization
Society, which tried to prevent indiscriminate relief from demoralizing
the casual poor. As her tenants were to be trained in self-help morality
by holding out the prospect of better housing as an instrument to
build character, so the cadets were to 'learn the duty and dignity of
obedience . . . get a sense of corporate life and of civic duty [and]
learn to honour the power of endurance and effort.'[48]

Working-class boys who joined the cadet movement were to receive
a new cultural identity through its 'unique and wonderful reforming
power', which would take them away from the 'temptations' of the
'undisciplined life' of the streets,[49] and facilitate their absorption into
a society dominated by middle class values:

The object of the Corps — to inculcate patriotism, discipline, and

habits of obedience to authority, self-reliance and regularity —
appealed to Miss Hill strongly, [wrote Lancelot Bennett in 1912,
not long after her death] *and fitted in with her general scheme*
for improving the welfare of her poorer neighbours.[50] (My italics)

An outmoded Victorian self-help, individualist ethic — of which by the
1900s Octavia Hill was an isolated defender — was to be instilled into
the potentially 'respectable' working class by the elevation of the moral
character of the upwardly aspiring.

It was claimed that over 1,000 cadets had passed from the 1st London
Cadet Battalion into the armed forces during the First World War,
but with the return to peace-time conditions, the strength of the
battalion was severly reduced. This was a reflection of the general
decline in cadet membership all over Britain as a result of financial
stringency and the wave of revulsion against military training experienced in the early 1920s.[51] The national total of army cadets did, in
fact, drop by over 58 per cent in this decade, from 118,893 in 1920 to
49,510 in 1928. There was also, during a period of ostensible internationalism and pacifism, a notable lethargy with regard to support
for cadet training at a local level. It was only the injection of some
fresh officer material in the 1920s — when Sherborne School in Dorset
sponsored two units attached to boys' clubs in London — that enabled
the original companies of the Southwark Cadet Corps to survive at all
in the inter-war period.[52] Even more serious for the cadet movement
were the effects on finance of the cavalier withdrawal by both Labour
and Conservative governments of the capitation grants awarded annually
to each cadet. Grants were first refused in 1923 as part of a government
economy measure; although in 1925 they were restored at the rate of
four shillings per cadet. Lord Derby, the Secretary of State for War,
then handed over the running of cadets — through the Territorials —
from the War Office to the Council of the County Territorial Army
Associations.[53]

Even worse was to follow for the beleagured and much diminished
'open' cadet units, now largely grouped in the industrial counties of
Warwickshire, Durham, Yorkshire and Lancashire. For without notice,
in 1930, official War Office 'recognition', together with arms and the
small capitation grant, were withdrawn by the Labour War Minister,
Tom Shaw. 'There is no connection between the Cadet Force and a
rabid militarism,' pleaded the *Sunday Times* vainly, 'Mr. Shaw might as
well prohibit the Salvation Army from wearing a uniform as penalise
the Cadets because they go in for physical drill on Army lines.'[54] The

immediate response to this government action from supporters of the
cadet movement was the formation, under Field-Marshal Lord Allenby,
of the British National Cadet Association, with a view to keeping the
Cadet Force alive by private subscription. Less than two years later,
however, recognition had been restored by the National Government and
the BNCA was made fully responsible for the organization and administration of the Cadet Force. But no grants were made available until
1937, when five shillings was paid for each cadet who met certain
military qualifications. At the outbreak of the Second World War,
the total strength of the Cadet Force was only about 20,000 but — as
it had done in 1899 and 1914 — war soon stimulated a considerable
expansion in numbers and, in order to deal with this, the War Office
took over control from the BNCA. Owing to the consequent shortage
of officers, the war saw the further disintegration of the 1st London
Cadet Battalion, as companies amalgamated or were temporarily
closed down or went out of existence altogether.[55]

In effect, the expansion of the cadet force during the war had been
preceded in 1941 by the Registration of Girls and Boys Order: a
government scheme under which all young people aged 16 or over had
to register with their local education authorities and, if not already a
member of a youth organization, were interviewed by a panel and ad-
vised, though not compelled, to join a suitable youth movement.[56]
One result of this spectacular wartime drive was that numbers in the
Cadet Force increased very rapidly to a mid-1945 total of 170,000. But
the problem of finding suitable officers remained acute and the Home
Guard was often called upon to help provide them. As the war went on,
the mobilization of cadets began to pay larger dividends: it is estimated
that by 1944 at least 40,000 ex-cadets were passing annually into the
ranks of the armed forces.[57]

After the war was over, the BNCA changed its title to the Army
Cadet Force and once again a considerable slackening of interest
followed as the nation began to concentrate its energies on peace-time
reconstruction and the building of a Welfare State. With the extension of
National Service to two years in 1950, cadet training was provided
with a much needed boost, while a War Office Report of 1957 led to
the movement becoming far more streamlined. Yet, since cadet forces
are in essence youth clubs in uniform financed by the tax-payer, in
the mid-1960s it was questioned whether spending money on 1,500
army cadet detachments with an average strength of 25 was at all
worthwhile. It was argued that the knowledge of Service life acquired in
a Cadet Force could be picked up more quickly and less expensively in

a month at a Service college or in a recruit unit.[58] As the links between
the Services and the general public became increasingly tenuous, the
post-1945 development of the Army Cadet Force has reflected its
position as a pre-Service voluntary organization sponsored by the Army
and closely affiliated to the local Territorials.

Notes

1.   Whereas one stream of cadets flows through the Public School cadet corps
       to the Junior Division of the Officer Training Corps (1908), to the Junior
       Training Corps (1939), to the present day Combined Cadet Force (1947);
       another emerges through the Church Lads' Brigade being handed over to
       the County Territorial Force Associations (1911), and the setting up by
       Lord Allenby of the British National Cadet Association (1930), changed
       to the present-day Army Cadet Force Association (1945).
2.   Derek Fraser, *The Evolution of the British Welfare State* (London, 1973),
       p. 121. Cf. C. L. Mowat, *The Charity Organization Society, 1869-1913*
       (London, 1961), *passim;* Harold Perkin, *The Origins of Modern English
       Society, 1780-1880* (London, 1969), p. 448; Gareth Stedman Jones,
       Outcast London (Oxford, 1971), chap. 14; Kathleen Woodroofe, *From
       Charity to Social Work: in England and the United States* (London, 1962),
       chap. 2.
3.   Volunteer battalions that raised their own locally recruited cadet companies
       in the early 1860s included: the Queen's Westminster Rifles (1860), the
       Huddersfield Volunteer Battalion (1862), the London Rifle Brigade (1860)
       and the South Middlesex Rifle Volunteers (1861). Cf. Anon. (W. L. New-
       combe), *The Army Cadet Force Handbook* (London, 1949), p. 14. There
       is some evidence that a few cadet corps were run for working-boy appren-
       tices in the iron foundries of Scotland and the North of England.
4.   See Lt.-Col. H. J. Harris, *A History of the First Hundred Years of the Rugby
       School Corps, 1860-1960* (Rugby, 1967), chap. 1. Information was also
       supplied by Hugh Cunningham, University of Kent.
5.   See Lt.-Col. H. C. Hughes, *The Army Cadets of Surrey, 1860-1960* (London,
       1960), pp. 2-3; Lt.-Col. H. C. Trist, *A Short History of the Rosall School
       Corps* (Fleetwood, 1960), *passim;* William Mc. G. Eager, *Making Men: a
       history of boys' clubs and related movements in Great Britain* (London,
       1953), pp. 313-318; Hugh Cunningham, *The Volunteer Force* (London,
       1975), p. 59.
6.   See Geoffrey Best, 'Militarism and the Victorian Public School' in Brian
       Simon and Ian Bradley (eds.), *The Victorian Public School* (Dublin, 1975),
       p. 136.
7.   See K. S. Inglis, *Churches and the Working Class in Victorian England*
       (London, 1963), chap. 4; W. Picht, *Toynbee Hall and the Settlement
       Movement* (London, 1914), *passim;* J. J. Mallon, 'The Story of Toynbee
       Hall' in *Social Service Review*, Vol. XX, No. 1 (Jan., 1939), pp. 19-24;
       J. A. R. Pimlott, *Toynbee Hall: fifty years of social progress, 1889-1934*
       (London, 1935), chap 11.
8.   Sir Francis Vane (1861-1934). See Biographical Notes.
9.   Cited in Pimlott, p. 78.
10.   See 'The Past Month' in *The Toynbee Record,* Vol. 1, No. 2 (Nov., 1888),
       p. 6. The Club, for sixteen to twenty-one year olds, was in Leman Street,

Whitechapel.

11.   See Sir Francis Vane, *Agin the Governments* (London, 1929), p. 63;
      Henry Nevinson, *Changes and Chances* (London, 1923), p. 95. Each
      recruit had to deposit 2/6d., which included a 6d. entrance fee.

12.   Nevinson, p. 91. After 1890, drill took place in Shadwell, at St Mary's
      House, Cable Street, near the London Dock basin. Nevinson was, at the
      time, a young associate member of Toynbee Hall, living with his wife in
      a set of workmen's flats in Whitechapel.

13.   William Ingham Brooke (18–1923). See Biographical Notes.

14.   The present Greater London Borough of Southwark, formed with the setting
      up of the Greater London Council in 1965, comprises the old London
      boroughs of Southwark, Rotherhithe, Bermondsey, Walworth, Camberwell,
      Peckham and Dulwich.

15.   See Anon., *The London Borough of Southwark Official Guide* (London,
      1973 edn.), pp. 13-29; Anon., (Mary Boast), *Southwark, A London Borough*
      (London, n.d.); F. Higham, *Southwark Story* (London, 1955); C. H.
      Blunden, *Riverside Story* (London, 1965).

16.   Geoffrey Best, *Temporal Pillars* (London, 1964), p. 492. From 1886 to
      1888, Octavia Hill, with the help of the Kyrle Society, converted a plot of
      land leased in a derelict condition from the Church Commissioners into an
      open space, to which cottages and a hall were later added. Cf. *Reports on
      the Red Cross Hall and Garden: 1895, 1899, 1900.* Southwark Public
      Library, Local History Collection.

17.   See Stedman Jones, *Outcast London,* p. 261.

18.   London Boys' clubs are listed in B. Paul Neuman, *The Boys' Club: in
      theory and practice* (London, 1900), pp. 44-61; C. R. B. Russell and L. M.
      Rigby, *Working Lads' Clubs* (London, 1908), appendix; *Report of the
      Federation of London Working Boys' Clubs and Institutes,* (1899, n.p.),
      B.M.

19.   Mrs. Russell Barrington, 'The Red Cross Hall' in *The English Illustrated
      Magazine,* Vol. X, No. 117 (June, 1893), p. 615. Cf. Anthony S. Wohl,
      'Octavia Hill and the Homes of the London Poor' in *The Journal of British
      Studies,* Vol. X, No. 2 (May, 1971), pp. 105-131; Geoffrey Best, pp. 488-
      496. Octavia Hill (1838-1912). See Biographical Notes.

20.   Cited in W. F. Airs and J. S. Streeter (eds.), *Sixty Years a Cadet, 1889-1949:
      a short history of the 1st London Cadet Battalion* (London, 1949), p. 5.
      Octavia Hill was, in any case, already familiar with the original East London
      Cadet Corps, for she quotes Canon Barnett approvingly as saying that, 'he
      thought there was nothing which could so gather in some of the most
      difficult rough boys, and do them so much good, as such a corps.' Hill,
      Letter to my Fellow Workers (London, 1888), p. 7.

21.   General Sir Garnet Wolseley agreed to take the Chair on the recommendation
      of Major-General Sir Frederick Maurice, a member of the Wolseley 'Ring',
      whose family had a close connection through marriage with the Hill family.
      See Octavia Hill to Sir Frederick Maurice, 30 March 1889, Wolseley Papers,
      Hove Library, Sussex. At the meeting, Wolseley made a point of stressing
      'the importance of cadet corps as providing a counter-attraction to public
      houses and music-halls.' The *Southwark Standard and South London News,*
      1 June 1889.

22.   Leaflet headed 'Southwark Cadet Corps', dated 1889, signed by Lord
      Wolmer, Octavia Hill and Ingham Brooke on behalf of the Red Cross Hall
      Committee. It also promised to provide, 'a sort of training school for
      recruits for the Army'. Ibid. Archives of C. Hoare's Bank, Fleet Street,
      London.

23.   Octavia Hill to Sir Frederick Maurice: (loc. cit.)

   It is proposed to try to interest the employers of labour and owners of
   property and other local magnates to help with funds, and with making
   the scheme known among their employees by inviting them to a meeting
   in the beautiful small hall we have built in Southwark.

24.   Cited: Octavia Hill to Lady Wolseley, 3 June 1889, Wolseley Papers.
25.   William George Cooper to A. W. Fisher, 12 May 1935, Petone, New Zealand:
        Library, Cadet Training Centre, Frimley Park, Camberley, Surrey. (Cooper,
        who joined the cadets in August 1889, was enrolled as a bookbinder in Ivy
        Lane.)
26.   Albert L. Salmond, Southwark Cadet Corps, 1st (Unofficial) *Annual Report*,
        2 June 1890, Red Cross Hall, n.p. Archives of Hoare's Bank.
27.   Viz., before 1914, companies in the 1st London Cadet Battalion were run
        by: the Oxford House Settlement on Bethnal Green; Eton College in Hack-
        ney; Harrow School in North Kensington; Haileybury School in Stepney and
        the Charterhouse School Mission. Clement Attlee, the future Labour
        Prime Minister, was commissioned a 2nd Lieutenant in the cadet company
        run by the Haileybury College Mission Club; while in 1911 his brother,
        Laurence, raised a new company for the Battalion in Islington. Cf. C. R.
        Attlee, *As it Happened* (London, 1956 edn.), p. 27.
28.   Under the War Office regulations of the 1880s, when a cadet unit
        reached the establishment strength of four companies, it could apply to be
        granted the status of an independent battalion of some Regular Army
        regiment. In competition with its rivals – units formed at Bermondsey
        (1885), Mayhall College, Herne Hill (1888) and Lambeth Polytechnic
        (1888) – the Southwark Cadet Corps won the race to acquire precedence
        and seniority over every other infantry cadet unit in the Army. See Anon.,
        *Notes on the History of the 1st Cadet Battalion, 'The Queen's' Royal
        Regiment, West Surrey, 1918-1944* (London, 1944), *passim.*, War Office
        Library; Lancelot Bennett, 'The Origins of the Army Cadet Force', in
        The Cadet Journal, Vol. IV, No. 6 (Nov., 1942), p. 151.
29.   Cf. Bibliography, Manuscript Collections: Cadet Training Centre; Guildhall
        Library; Hoare's Bank; Institute of Civil Engineers; North Cadbury; Stoke
        Newington; Winterborne Zelston.
30.   See Octavia Hill, *Letter to My Fellow Workers* (London, 1890), p. 10.
        The early records of the Battalion abound with reports of such important
        events in the ceremonial calendar as the annual Military Exhibition, a pre-
        decessor of the Royal Tournament, and the Lord Mayor's Show.
31.   Albert Salmond, (–1902). See Biographical Notes.
32.   Sydney Cockerell (1867-1962). See Biographical Notes.
33.   Lancelot Bennett (1865-1949). See Biographical Notes.
34.   Anon., 'Camp at Aldershot', reprinted from the *Pall Mall Gazette*, 20
        August 1891, p.3.
35.   This is largely explained by the long association of printing and book-
        binding with the City of London and Southwark. The strongholds of the
        trade clustered around Blackfriars Bridge, viz., in Fleet Street, Farringdon
        Street and Stamford Street: all within walking distance of the boys' homes
        in, for example, Union Street, Borough High Street and the Old Kent Road.
36.   Source: *1st Cadet Battn., 'The Queen's', Royal West Surrey Regiment
        Enrolment Book*, May 1889-June 1891. Library, Cadet Training Centre.
37.   Letter from Bennett, 7 May 1904, *Report of the Physical Deterioration
        Committee*, P.O., 1904 (Cd. 2210), Vol. XXXII, Appendix XXII, p. 86.

38. See *Report on hours and conditions of employment of van boys and ware-house boys.* Dept. Committee, PP, 1913 (Cd. 6886), Vol. XXXIII.

39. See Gareth Stedman Jones, *Outcast London,* pp. 69-71.

40. 'Occupations of Cadets at Date of Enrolment', Bennett, Mins. of Evidence, Appendix XXIII, Table II, pp. 87-88. For reasons of comparison this table has been amended so as not to include data for 1902 or for the Pimlico area given in the original.

41. See Cyril Jackson, *Report on Boy Labour,* Appendix Vol. XX, *Royal Commission on the Poor Laws,* PP, 1901 (Cd. 4632), XLIV, pp. 204-205. Another 18 per cent entered skilled trades (only 4 per cent in printing), 14 per cent became shop boys and 8 per cent office boys or junior clerks in occupations providing solely for juvenile employment. Cf. Reginald Bray, *Boy Labour and Apprenticeship* (London, 1911), pp. 114-118.

42. See Stedman Jones, p. 70. Such was the habitually short-term market for juvenile labour and the inelastic demand for unskilled teenagers that, of those who gained employment between 10 and 14 in such jobs, the majority tended to lose them anyway between the ages of 18 and 25, or else they left to find employment in another form of unskilled labour which paid more adult wage rates.

43. At the age of 17, of 519 boys entering the Army in 1909: low-skilled = 48%; general and casual = 12%; shop boys = 10%; skilled = 6% and clerical = 5%. As a total of the 14 to 20 age band: skilled and clerical = 33% and low-skilled and unskilled = 67%. See Cyril Jackson, Table 25, p. 54.

44. The Annual Report for 1891 of the 1st London Cadet Battalion mentions 193 recruits being sent to the Services since the Battalion was formed: 61 as Guards and Infantry of the line; 45 as Militia; and 53 as Volunteers. During the Boer War, large numbers of ex-Southwark Cadets went into the City of London Imperial Volunteers or the 2nd Battalion, 'The Queen's'.

45. Bennett cited in Airs and Streeter, *Sixty Years a Cadet,* p. 12.

46. Ibid., p. 19.

47. Octavia Hill, *Our Common Land and other short essays* (London, 1877), p. 97. She felt that working-class boys were 'cowardly and wanting in power of endurance, wanting in power of standing together, worshippers of money.' Octavia Hill to her mother, 19 May 1889, cited: C. Edmund Maurice (ed.), *Life of Octavia Hill as told in her letters* (London, 1913), p. 492.

48. Octavia Hill, *Letter to My Fellow Workers* (London, 1910), pp. 11-12. 'And if such ideals can be brought before the young lad before he gets in with a gang of loafers it may make all the difference to his life.' Ibid.

49. Ibid., 1909, pp. 12-13.

50. Lancelot Bennett, 'Miss Octavia Hill and Cadets', *The Times,* 19 August 1912. 'Moreover, she hoped, and it has been amply verified, that the working boy would cultivate, by means of these cadet companies, the spirit of comradeship and *esprit de corps* which is so marked a trait in his more fortunate public school brother.' Ibid.

51. J. Veysey, who ran a company of the Church Lads' Brigade in Lewisham from the mid-1930s, remembers plainly that the CLB nearly became extinct in the 1920s 'because of the almost hysterical revulsion against militarism.' Interview recorded on 20 September 1971 in Brenchley, Kent. (The CLB until 1936 was an integral part of the national cadet force.)

52. Colonel Bennett, himself an Old Shirburnian, first approached the Head-master of Sherbourne School and, after much negotiation, the School and Old Shirburnian Society agreed to sponsor 'B' Company in Southwark in 1921 and 'A' Company in 1925. By the mid-1930s, the school's mission or boys' club in Southwark was 'going through a very thin patch'. See *Report*

of Meeting at Sherborne of Old Shirburnian Society to consider the present state of affairs at Sherborne House, 3 March 1935: collection of Col. R. D. Sherbrooke-Walker, North Cadbury, Somerset.

53.   See Lieut.-Col. H. C. Hughes, *The Army Cadets of Surrey, 1860-1960* (London, 1960), pp. 8-9.

54.   The *Sunday Times*, 2 November 1930. The only reluctant concession obtained was that the date of non-recognition was deferred from 1 April (only seven days' notice) to 31 October 1930; which gave the CCTA seven months grace in which to wind up all their cadet commitments.

55.   The 1940s saw the virtual disappearance of the 1st London Cadet Battalion as a self-sufficient entity, but it remained a battalion with two companies each in Southwark and Islington. In 1957 Sherborne School took 'A' and 'B' companies from Southwark to boys' clubs in Bermondsey: 'B' became a Royal Marine Cadet Unit of the Sea Cadet Corps and 'A' a Royal Artillery Unit. By the early 1970s, the former had closed down and there were plans to use Sherborne House Boys' Club in Bermondsey for the after-care training of ex-prisoners. Only one company of the original 1st London still survives – 'G' Company in Stoke Newington – but in Greater London alone there are over one hundred cadet companies attached to other battalions.

56.   One writer remembers, 'with what trepidation he went to that interview – what a frightful bore to have to go to a youth club once a week.' John Wakelin, *et. al., Responsibility for Youth* (London, 1961), p. 18. Accounts differ as to how much 'pressure' was brought to bear upon young people to join a youth movement.

57.   See Anon. (W. L. Newcombe), *The Army Cadet Force Handbook* (London, 1949), p. 20.

58.   See Frank Dawes, 'The high price of playing soldiers', the *Sun*, 18 March 1967. In the late 1960s there were about 39,000 Army Cadets, 17,800 Sea Cadets and 28,000 in the Air Training Corps – all for boys who had left school before the age of 17. The 1975 strength of the Army Cadet Force was: 2,857 officers, 3,652 adult instructors, 38,663 cadets and 1,600 detachments.

5 LOCAL YOUTH IN UNIFORM

One way of finding out how youth movements fared in practice, more precisely than if they are seen solely from the point of view of their founders' theoretical intentions, is to investigate more closely particular organizations in a particular locality. Enfield in North London has been chosen for this scrutiny, not simply because of the survival of records relating to local Boys' Brigade companies and Boy Scout troops, but also for its interesting social and economic history between 1880 and 1914. Actually situated in the County of Middlesex, Enfield grew – within the space of two or three generations – from a small market town on the outskirts of a spreading metropolis into a thriving dormitory or commuter suburb. Enfield is an exception to the general rule of London suburban development in the last quarter of the nineteenth century, however, since as part of the industrialized North East 'quadrant' of London, it became an industrial as well as a middle-class residential suburb.[1]

The transition from country town to suburb of London accelerated in the 1880s with the building of speculative housing estates to accommodate the large London 'overspill', arriving to work in the new factories springing up like mushrooms along the Lea Valley in East Enfield. This expansion had been pioneered by the Royal Small Arms Factory in the mid-nineteenth century.[2] But it was the transfer of Edison and Swan's famous electric light-bulb company from Newcastle to Ponders End in 1886 that opened up the district by bringing employment to thousands, marking the beginnings of large scale modern industrial development.[3] The urban growth of Enfield and neighbouring Edmonton was also facilitated by railway development outpacing canal traffic, while a reservoir of skilled and semi-skilled labour attracted new industry to the superficially unpromising Lea Valley – with its windswept marshes, flanked by fields, in the 'still primordial bleakness of the Middlesex scene.'[4] After about 1880, industrial growth paralleled urbanization and population expansion as the eastern parts of the two parishes were transformed into virtual working-class enclaves.

The social geography of Enfield reflects the cruciform pattern which has been discerned for Greater London,[5] with the middle classes living on the higher, better drained ground along the residential areas whose very names suggest height (the Ridgeway, Clay Hill, Windmill Hill and Winchmore Hill), while the working classes were to be found clustered around the low-lying, unhealthy, marshy areas of the Lea Valley adjacent to industry in places such as Enfield Wash, Enfield Highway, Enfield Lock and Ponders End. If the Thames is the chief architect of London, then the Lea — joining him in Poplar — is his main assistant. The social geography of Enfield is not quite this straight-forward, for imposed upon the cruciform pattern was an east-west social division. To the east of the railway lines from central London along the banks of the Lea were the industrial working-class housing estates, while to the west were the more middle-class and lower-middle-class residential areas, eventually extending to Southgate and East Barnet.[6] The introduction in 1872 by the Great Eastern Railway of trains offering a cheap two-penny workman's return fare, attracted large numbers of working men to the Lea Valley, from which they could travel to their places of work in the City or the East End of London.[7]

Such, briefly, is the local context within which the nationally organized and centralized youth movements known as the Boys' Brigade and the Boy Scouts are to be set. The first Boys' Brigade company to appear in Enfield was started in 1888: one of the earliest and, sub-sequently, most famous companies to appear in London.[8] A prominent local Nonconformist, the Enfield Medical Officer of Health, Dr J. J. Ridge,[9] was originally responsible for bringing William Smith's idea to Enfield; seeing it as a solution to his problems of Sunday School discipline.[10] Despite a nervous manner, Ridge preached the Gospel in the open air after Services on Sunday evenings, until in 1885 he helped to set up the Mission Church — sponsored by a wealthy Congregation-alist 'Mother Church' a few minutes' walk away — which was to become the home of the 1st Enfield Company.[11] The Brigade thus began its activities in one of the poorer districts of North Enfield, repeating a pattern of working among the 'deserving' poor started in Glasgow. Unlike William Smith, however, Dr Ridge was uncompromising both in his Evangelism and in his teetotalism. As Superintendent of the Mission's Sunday School, he became the first Captain of the Company, although, drill never being one of his strongest points, he soon handed over the post to the eighteen-year-old son of the Mother Church's Minister.

On 31 October, 1890, a second company of the Boys' Brigade was started in Enfield by the Congregationalists in Bush Hill Park.[12] Originally an exclusive district of timbered park-land, formerly the estate of the Mellish family, in the 1880s a dense colony of cheaper houses were erected here as a piece of land speculation to provide small, self-contained houses at cheap rents for the Lea Valley's influx

of industrial workers. This company met in the 'Avenue Hall' Mission
Church, a corrugated iron building which had been erected a few years
previously by middle-class Evangelicals from the more 'respectable' side
of the railway line – running from Liverpool Street to Enfield Town –
which effectively bisected Bush Hill Park socially.[13] The original
Captain of the 2nd Enfield was a founder and Deacon of the Mission
Church in Bush Hill Park: Henry S. Hardman, a local builder and
property developer who had won a seat as a Liberal on Enfield Urban
District Council. In the 1900s, the Captain of the Company was Martin
Jenkins, the son of a local dentist, who owned a printing business in
Watford and lived in one of the cottages associated with Charles Lamb.[14]

A few months later, the 3rd Enfield Boys' Brigade Company was set
up at Christ Church itself.[15] Their first Captain was Norris Toms, the
second eldest son of the Minister, aided initially by a Church member.
During this company's second session, Toms invited Thomas R. Plowman,
whose family owned a large brick-making business in Tottenham and
Edmonton, to take over as Captain – although he was only 16 at the
time. Plowman filled the position admirably, it would appear, until
his premature death in 1920.[16] These early Enfield companies received
financial support from rich local Nonconformists, such as George
Spicer, who lived on the Ridgeway, a much respected member of the
paper-manufacturing family. It was a great occasion when he made his
weekly visit to the area, always arriving promptly in his horse-drawn,
two-wheel gig, driven by a chauffeur, for meetings of the Pleasant Sunday
Afternoon Club, of which he was Chairman.[17]

A Nonconformist urban élite drawn, like these early Boys' Brigade
Captains, from the ranks of the professional or entrepreneurial middle
classes, dominated the early history of the Brigade in Enfield through an
inter-locking web of family relationships and religious connections. The
strength of the Free Church chapels, rapidly springing up in the suburbs,
and often carrying more weight in working-class districts than the old
Anglican establishment, lay not simply in numbers, but also in their
ability to organize and lead a pressure group whose urban programme
they legitimized on religious grounds and pressed on the amorphous
Liberal Party of the late-nineteenth century.[18] The Boys' Brigade
emerged in Enfield at the same time as the local Nonconformist leadership was strengthening its grip on local politics and culture. Prominent
figures on the expanding suburban scene, motivated very often by a
puritan-like zeal, tempered by radicalism, the Congregationalists and
Unitarians were usually the chief promoters of middle-class progres-
sivism.[19] They promulgated suburban middle-class values while stead-

fastly rejecting immigrant working-class leisure activities.

In Bush Hill Park, chapel provided a primary source of recreational
amusement: in the form of Sunday School Classes filled to over-
flowing, Pleasant Sunday Afternoon musical meetings, a Gospel Temperance Society, Bible Classes and much-anticipated annual outings.[20]
The village-community way of life still persisted in this working-class
enclave of Enfield. Within a framework of urban leisure dominated by
religious provision, the Boys' Brigade became, at first, simply one more
extension of the 'Institutional Church' idea systematically fostered by
Congregationalism, as a method of attracting the widest possible church
membership.[21] At the same time, the Boys' Brigade in Enfield represented the alien intrusion of a military discipline and militant Evangelism that owed more to a revivalist Scottish Presbyterianism than to
suburban middle-class English Nonconformity.

Known until a battalion was formed in 1903 as 'The United Enfield
Companies', the local Boys' Brigade soon settled down into a weekly
routine of drill, Bible Class and Club Room, disturbed only by military
inspections, athletic competitions and the occasional concert or field
day.[22] The persecution of roving bands of 'hooligans' made the friendly
rivalry between the early companies almost mandatory as a form of
survival against a hostile environment, for 'it was a long time before
Drill and other gatherings could be held without the risk of interruption
from rowdies outside.'[23]

In the pre-1914 years of the Boys' Brigade in Enfield, company rules
were strictly exercised, thus reinforcing the authority of other adult
figures with power over the young, such as school-teachers and police-
men, in creating 'a general atmosphere of being controlled which led
to discipline.'[24] In 1910, for example, Dr R. Leslie Ridge, a son of the
Battalion's founder, dealt with one potential 'mutiny' in the 1st Enfield
— of which he was Captain — by simply dismissing all 19 'demonstrators'
from the Company. The effect of this sort of treatment is difficult to
gauge, but as Dr Ridge declared, 'from that time onwards, the Company
knew what "Discipline" meant.'[25] One departing Band Sergeant confessed:

People who knew me five years ago do not know me as the same chap
now, I reckon, and I don't mind saying so, I was one of the biggest
little blackguards in Enfield, but the Company has turned me out
— what I am now. Do your duty to the Company. I am sorry I am
leaving.[26]

Table 1: Enrolment in 1st Enfield Co. Boys' Brigade[27]

Occupation	Enrolment 1893-1894	%	Alphabetical Admissions 1890-1908	%
Schoolboy	13	11	59	37
Shopboy	12	10	18	11
Paperboy	15	12	7	4½
Houseboy	14	11	11	7
Edison & Swan	13	11	8	5
Milkboy	5	4	7	4½
Building	7	6	8	5
Clerical	7	6	8	5
Skilled	7	6	6	4
Messenger boy	3	2	5	3
Factory Worker	5	4	-	-
Shop Assistant	6	5	6	4
Printers' boy	4	3	4	3
Gardeners	3	2	2	1
Farm workers	2	1	3	2
Unclassified	7	6	6	4
Totals	123	100	158	100

These early companies of the Boys' Brigade in Enfield recruited largely from errand boys or schoolboys, with a noticeable contingent from the recently opened Edison and Swan's factory in Ponders End (Table 1). One explanation for the hostility towards the Boys' Brigade aroused among those who did not join was the aura of social respectability surrounding boys who attended Sunday School and later compulsory Bible Class.

> Few drills went by without attacks from hooligans and the 'discontents' [remembered one Captain] even officers in uniform were pelted with bottles and other missiles as they went to drill, and the boys had to defend their uniform often with their fists.[28]

The officers were drawn from the ranks of the professional and property-owning 'bourgeoisie' whose social status was often incumbent upon the

performance of community service. 'The whole idea of the Boys'
Brigade, when it was founded,' explained J. J. Ridge's grandson, 'was to
be officered by the sons of "gentlemen", as they used to say in those
days.'[29] After the First World War, the participation of what were
known as the 'varsity and public-school 'types' diminished, until
today recruitment for officers in the Boys' Brigade comes almost over-
whelmingly from the ranks.[30]

Twenty years after the appearance of the Boys' Brigade in Enfield,
the Boy Scouts made their entrance into this populous suburban
setting. The majority of the early Scout troops in London were attached
to Anglican churches. They came garlanded with all the glamour of
novelty and the heroic charisma of Baden-Powell to assist them in
drawing recruits away from their Nonconformist rival, the Boys' Brigade.
Scouting took root rapidly in North London, especially in Highgate,
Holloway, Highbury and Islington, before extending further out into
predominantly working-class areas such as Tottenham and Edmonton,
then eventually to Enfield. But it was not until October 1919 that,
largely for the sake of administrative convenience, Enfield officially
became a member of the North London District Scout Council.[31] One
of the earliest troops to be registered in London was also the first troop
of Boy Scouts in Enfield. It originated one evening in March 1908,
when half a dozen 'factory boys' called on the Revd A. R. Browne,
newly created Curate of St James' Anglican Church at Ponders End,
produced the fortnightly four-penny parts of *Scouting for Boys* and
asked him to be their Scoutmaster.[32] Renting their headquarters over
a local grocer's shop, the enthusiasm of the original members proved
contagious. According to the Revd Browne:

> They started work in the factories at 7.30 a.m. and kept on to early
> evening, which left them little time for Scouting. But in order to get
> their training they came along at 5.00 a.m. and trained in the lanes
> around here before they started work.[33]

During the early months of Scouting in Enfield, the Revd Browne
constantly had to march the Troop out under a hail of stones, jeers and
threats from other boys,[34] that recalls the initial reception accorded to
the Boys' Brigade. Yet by Christmas 1908, the 1st Enfield Highway
Troop were 40 strong and a few months later could afford to set up a
forerunner of the Wolf Cubs for boys under twelve.[35] In 1913, Browne,
then the acknowledged leader of Scouting in Enfield, migrated to South
Africa, but he left behind him a strong local association which he had

helped to set up in 1910. However chequered their subsequent careers, several other Boy Scout troops soon got off the ground in Enfield.[36] But the troop about which most information has survived prior to 1914 is the 5th Enfield Troop, which was started about a year after the Revd Browne's first successful experiment.[37] On 29 July 1909, Percy Bantock Nevill,[38] a young articled accountant on the way to an audit, picked up a cheap paper-bound edition of *Scouting for Boys* on a station book-stall in Coventry and was almost instantaneously converted to the move-ment to which he was to devote the rest of his life.[39] Nevill decided to form his own troop in Enfield since none of the others already active in the area required his assistance. He was put in touch with the Revd Browne in his capacity as the local Secretary of Boy Scouts in Enfield. On 2 October 1909, Nevill arranged a meeting to appeal for recruits, defining the goals of Scouting as, 'to make good citizens and to foster the spirit of patriotism in the boys of our Empire.'[40]

In the beginning, the working-class boys of Enfield flocked to join th exciting new game 'invented' by the Hero of Mafeking. Yet if the 5th Enfield's records can be taken as at all representative, disillusion soon followed upon the discovery that it was often too expensive a game for the sons of unemployed or unskilled workers to play. 'Poor boys didn't gravitate to Baden-Powell's movement . . . the very poor hadn't money to spare for jersey and hat and belt, to say nothing of the subs.'[41] This was at a time when the purchasing power of wages was declining as food prices outstripped incomes.[42] On 22 July 1910, Scout Harrington wrote to Nevill asking to leave the Troop:

> on account of not being unable [*sic*] to leave work in time. And another thing I find it too expensive, as dad is out of work , and all my Pocket money goeing towards home. I am sending my nick's back, and shirt as well.[43]

Despite such early defections, the 5th Enfield managed to survive, largely because, given its socially variegated catchment area in Bush Hill Park,[44] there was always some continuity of middle-class and lower-middle-class membership.[45] Gradually, under Nevill's inspired leader-ship, the 5th Enfield became a distinctive force in North London Scout-ing. If his speeches merely reflected Baden-Powell's exhortations, in practice Nevill's genuine idealism found expression in dedicated hard work for the movement. Equally, one cannot afford to overlook the pleasure and sense of release from urban, parental and occupational constraints which Scouting represented before 1914 for the schoolboys and errand boys of Enfield.

If the accounts of their week-end activities written by the Boy Scouts themselves should be treated with some caution — since they were written to receive the Scoutmaster's approval — they do at least indicate a sense of the enjoyment taken in 'playing the game'. The reports submitted by the 5th Enfield Boy Scouts of, for example, the County Rally of Middlesex Scouts on 22 February 1911, or of various annual camps held from 1910 to 1914,[46] make it abundantly clear that Scoutmaster Nevill interpreted the movement's handbook, *Scouting for Boys*, according to his own boy-centred outlook. He was anxious to recreate the same blend of open-air games, sing-songs, prayers and services he had first encountered in 1902 while attending a public-school Boys' Camp.[47] And for his Assistant Scoutmasters, it appears that Nevill only selected, 'public-school men of the very best type.'[48] Together they ran a Club Room for the Troop with various activities taking place on *every* night of the week.[49] To become Patrol Leaders or Seconds, Boy Scouts had to pass either their First or Second Class badge tests; they could then go on to take the various proficiency badges available, climaxed by the King's Scout Badge.[50]

When the First World War broke out, the 5th Enfield Troop were in camp between Enfield and Potters' Bar, since camping on the Isle of Wight had been prohibited by the British government.[51] Scoutmaster Nevill was prevented by poor eyesight from enlisting, so he divided his time energetically between Enfield and East London where, in 1915, he started the 22nd Poplar Boy Scouts in a notoriously 'rough' area. Earlier, in an atmosphere of patriotic 'good turns' performed by Boy Scouts, Nevill had offered his Enfield Troop's assistance in running a night-shift canteen organized by Lady Lawrence for the workers at the Royal Small Arms munitions factory in Enfield Lock.[52] Sadly, during the course of the bloody conflict that followed, several members of Nevill's Boy Scout Troop were killed in action, the toll being particularly high among those who joined the Navy or the Merchant Marine.[53] It is a telling reflection of the death rate during this war that it should have decimated such a representative social group of young men.

What does this account of both Scouting and the Boys' Brigade in Enfield before 1914 tell us about youth movements in general at a local level? It suggests, first of all, that the majority of the officers, whether Nonconformist or Anglican, were drawn from the public-school educated, professional or employer middle class. At least until the 1920s, Scoutmasters and Boys' Brigade Captains came from the ranks of the well-off, well-educated with the leisure and money to spare, whereas the boys were much more likely to come from a wider occupational spread. It is noticeable that the 1st Enfield Boys' Brigade Company included a larger number of errand boys and houseboys than the 1st Glasgow Company examined earlier. But the social diversity of the 5th Enfield Boy Scouts may reflect more the social geography of Bush Hill Park than the typical Scout recruitment pattern. Experience in Enfield also suggests that, at least in the case of the Boys' Brigade, a few prominent Nonconformist families — the Ridges, Toms and Plowmans — could effectively dominate the movement locally both as leaders and as participants. Religious affiliation was also a prerequisite for a Scoutmaster, but it was Church attendance rather than any part-icular denomination that was encouraged.

Notes

1. The North East industrial 'quadrant' takes in Walthamstow, Tottenham and Edmonton along the Lea Valley manufacturing belt. See J. Morris, 'The Development of Industries since the 18th Century', 21 December 1966, paper in Edmonton Public Library; Enfield District Manufacturers' Assoc-iation, *Industries of Enfield* (Enfield, 1930), chap. 3.

2. See Enfield Archaeological Society, Research Report No. 2, *Industrial Archaeology in Enfield: a survey of industrial monuments in the London Borough of Enfield* (Enfield, 1971), pp. 8-12; Ian Hay, *'R.O.F.' Story of the Royal Ordnance Factories, 1939-1948* (London, HMSO, 1949), p. 12; Guy R. Williams, *London in the Country: the growth of suburbia* (London, 1975), pp. 47-50.

3. See Anon., *The Pageant of the Lamp: the story of the electric lamp* (London, 1950), *passim;* 'Townsman' (Leo A. Eastwick), *Enfield Gazette,* 2 May, 9 May 1969. 'Almost the first thought of young wage earners leaving school was to seek an opening at "The Light".' Ibid.

4. Anon., *The Pageant of the Lamp*, p. 39.

5. Peter Wilmott and Michael Young, 'The Great Cross of London' in the *Sunday Times Magazine,* 22 October 1972, pp. 65-66; *idem., The Symmetrical Family* (Pelican edn., 1975), pp. 50-58.

6. See Alan A. Jackson, *Semi-Detached London: suburban development, life and transport, 1900-1939* (London, 1973), chap. 4.

7. The Great Eastern had been obliged to put on the cheap trains in return for displacing workers during the building of the Liverpool Street terminus in the 1860s. The Liverpool Street line had been extended to Enfield in 1849 but the Great Northern did not open up an alternative route from Kings Cross to Enfield Chase until 1871.

8. Sources for 1st Enfield Company: Anon. (Dr R. Leslie Ridge), 'Bits of Company History', Vol. XXII, Nos. 2-14, *1st Enfield Co. Magazine* (September 1942-March 1943); *idem.,* '1st. Enfield BB Co.' in *The Enfield Battalion Souvenir Handbook, 1888-1948* (Enfield, 1948), p. 2; holograph drafts of annual reports, 1907-1915, in possession of present Captain, L. R. Moody, Enfield.

9. Dr John James Ridge (1847-1908). See Biographical Notes.

10. Dr Ridge first heard about the Boys' Brigade through a supplement to the

Sunday School Chronicle, 11 May 1888, which discussed the pros and cons of the movement, reporting the reaction to a paper by William Smith. See Alan J. Ridge, 'The Early History of the 1st Enfield', holograph MS., (n.d.), p. 1, in possession of ex-Captain E. J. Berkelmans, South Woodford, London.

11.   See G. W. Knight, *Nonconformist Churches in Enfield* (Enfield, 1973), p. 7; J. S. Stribling, *A History of Christ Church Enfield, 1780-1917* (Enfield, 1917), p. 20; Anon., *Christ Church Manual,* (Enfield, 1911), p. 40. The 1911-1918 Baptismal Roll shows that there were a large number of labourers, railway workers, building workers and gardeners, attending the Mission, which in 1938 became a Congregational Church.

12.   See Henry S. Hardman, 'Congregationalism at Bush Hill Park', *Enfield Chronicle,* 5 December 1902; *Minute Book, Avenue Hall Congregational Church Committee, 1892-1904, Enfield*; Anon., (Charles Wright), *Jubilee Scrapbook, facts, scraps, odds and ends, bearing on the History, Life and Progress of the 2nd. Company of the Enfield Battalion of the Boys' Brigade,* type-written Ms. (1940), 55 pp.

13.   The London Road side of Bush Hill Park contained sedate villas, while across the railroad-bridge were the 'Avenues', small shops and two-up-two-down terraced housing, now rapidly being demolished to be replaced by impersonal, small-scale blocks of flats. See 'Townsman' (Leo. A. Eastwick), 'Days of the "Avenues" are Numbered', *Enfield Gazette,* 24 November 1972.

14.   Information on early Captains from: ex-Captain E. A. Sweetman, interviewed 20 September 1974; Captain Nix, 2nd Enfield, interviewed 10 September 1974.

15.   Sources for 3rd Enfield Company: Charles Chopping, *Some Records in the History of the 3rd, from 'records' and memory,* September 1963, type-written Ms., in possession of Mr Fred Gould, Enfield; *Annual Reports of the 1st and 3rd Enfield Companies, 1908-1910.*

16.   See Obituary, *Enfield Gazette and Observer,* 2 January 1920; Biographical Sketch, ibid., 9 January 1920, p. 7.

17.   See Peter Law, 'Where Archie Adams spent his Boyhood', *Enfield Gazette,* 27 April 1973.

18.   See Revd J. H. S. Kent, 'The Role of Religion in the Cultural Structure of the Later Victorian City', *Transactions of the Royal Historical Society,* 5th series, Vol. XXIII (1973), p. 156.

19.   Viz., in 1904 prominent local Congregationalists, such as Dr J. J. Ridge, Revd H. S. Toms, and T. R. Plowman, refused to pay part of their Poor Rates as an act of 'passive resistance' to the 1902 Education Act which compelled them to support Voluntary Church Schools from the rates. See 'Passive Resisters at Enfield', *Meyer's Observer,* 25 March 1904; *Enfield and Edmonton Chronicle,* ibid.; Log Book of Bush Hill Park 'Avenue Hall' Mission Church, 20 July 1930; Hugh McLeod, *Class and Religion in the Late Victorian City* (London, 1974), p. 178; J. E. Munson, 'A Study of Nonconformity in Edwardian England as revealed by the passive resistance movement against the 1902 Education Act', D.Phil. thesis, University of Oxford, 1973.

20.   See F. Garrett, 'Sixty Years of Sunday School Work' in E. G. Amos (ed.), Bush Hill Park Congregational Church Sunday School Enfield, *Diamond Jubilee Brochure,* (Enfield, 1947), pp. 5-9; 'Townsman' (Leo A. Eastwick), 'From Bush Hill Park to Theydon Bois by Brake in 1908', *Enfield Gazette,* 27 July 1973; Trevor Blackwell, 'The History of a Working Class Methodist Chapel, 1885-1970' in *Working Papers in Cultural Studies,* No. 5 (Spring,

1   Sir William Alexander Smith, founder of the Boys' Brigade, in
his thirty-ninth year, wearing the uniform of an officer in the 1st.
Lanarkshire Rifle Volunteers.

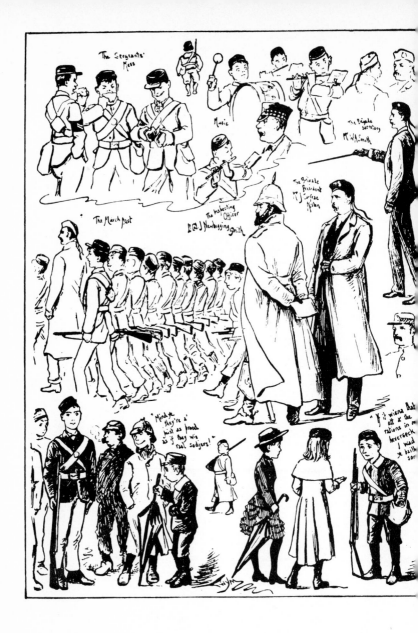

2   Drawings of probably the earliest Parade and Inspection of the Glasgow
Battalion of the Boys' Brigade, held at Burnbank during the spring holiday o
1886. William Smith is the full-length figure portrayed in the top right-hand
section. Note the Glaswegian dialect employed in the lower sections.

3 *(above)* A group photograph of the 3rd. Hamilton (Scotland) Company of the Boys' Brigade, identified by the 3H on their 'pill-box' caps, circa 1890. On one side of the burly Captain *(centre)* is his First Lieutenant, on the other the Presbyterian Captain to the Company. Note the simple uniform of belt and white haversack worn over the boy's ordinary working clothes, the dummy rifles and flutes.

4 *(below)* Boy Scouts belonging to the 1st. Enfield Highway Troop with *(centre)* their Scoutmaster, the Revd A. R. Browne, young Curate of St James' Anglican Church. This photograph was taken outside their headquarters, rented over a local grocer's shop in Ponders End, near Enfield, circa 1909.

5   Boy Scouts belonging to the Kangaroo Petrol *(see pennants)* of the 5th. Enfield Troop in Bush Hill Park, with *(rear)* their Scoutmaster, Percy Bantock Nevill, and in early Guide uniform *(centre)* his sister, posing for the camera in the Middlesex countryside, circa 1910.

6a   *(above right)* One of the buglers in the breakaway Brotherhood of British Boy Scouts, led by P.H. Pooley, circa 1920. Contrast the more elaborate appendages worn on this uniform with that of the mainstream Boy Scouts.

6b   *(bottom left)* A 'tall, well set-up young Citizen Soldier' or cadet of the 1st. Cadet Battalion, the King's Royal Rifle Corps, to which the Church Lads' Brigade was affiliated, in full marching order uniform before 1914.

CADET. FULL MARCHING ORDER.
1ST C.B. KING'S ROYAL RIFLE CORPS.

WILL YOU HELP US TO TURN
THESE

INTO

THIS?

IF SO

PLEASE FILL UP AND RETURN THE FOR[M]
ON OPPOSITE PAGE.

PUNCH, OR THE LONDON CHARIVARI—September 1, 1909.

OUR YOUNGEST LINE OF DEFENCE.

Boy Scout (to Mrs. Britannia). "FEAR NOT, GRAN'MA; NO DANGER CAN BEFALL YOU NOW. REMEMBER, I AM WITH YOU!"

7   *(above left)* A Church Lads' Brigade leaflet of the 1890's that set
out to attract subscriptions by its emphasis on the movement's potential
as an agency of social discipline.

8   *(below left)* 'Our Youngest Line of Defence'. The celebrated *Punch*
illustration by Bernard Partridge, linking Scouting with national defence
at the time of the Crystal Palace Rally of Boy Scouts in September 1909.

9   *(above)* A 'tug-of-war' between the sexes in a Woodcraft Folk Camp
near Sheffield, circa 1935, which, unlike the more traditional youth
movements, highlights their co-educational basis. Note the fringed jerkin
uniform *(centre)* and the distinctive badge worn on the breast of certain
onlookers.

10   Walter Mallock Gee, Secretary and founder of the Church Lads'
Brigade, in the uniform of a Colonel in the Brigade.

1974), pp. 65-84; Kenneth Young, *Chapel: the joyous days and prayerful nights of the Nonconformist in their heyday, c. 1850-1950* (London, 1972), chap. 4.

21.   See R. Tudor Jones, *Congregationalism in England, 1662-1962* (London, 1962), p. 297, pp. 315-319; Charles Silvester Horne, *The Institutional Church* (London, 1906), *passim*.

22.   See 'The Boys' Brigade: Battalion Inspection and Sports', the *Enfield Observer*, 31 May 1912, 9 June 1911; 'First Enfield Company at the Bycullah Athenaeum', ibid., 9 June 1914. The 1st Enfield had an enviable record for winning bugle, band and drill competitions in the London District; while between 1906-1919 the 3rd Enfield Co. was constantly winning the *Daily Telegraph* competition for the most efficient all-round company of the Boys' Brigade. See 'Enfield Company triumphs at London B.B. Display' in *Enfield Gazette*, 18 May 1973.

23.   Alan J. Ridge, 'Early History of the 1st Enfield Co.' p. 3.

24.   Cited: interview with E. A. Sweetman.

25.   Anon. (Dr R. Leslie Ridge), 'Bits of Company History', in *1st Enfield Company Magazine* Vol. XXII, No. 11 (Jan., 1943), n.p. The 'mutiny' was most probably a result of his strictly enforced rules that N.C.O.s were not allowed girl-friends. Those dismissed were only allowed to re-enrol on condition that they signed a declaration of loyalty.

26.   Band Sergeant G. Wilson Leave Taking Speech, *N.C.O.s Speeches*, typescript, 27 May 1912, in possession of E. A. Sweetman.

27.   Sources: *Enrolment Book of 1st. Enfield Co., 1893-1894*, in possession of present Captain, L. R. Moody; *1st. Enfield Co. Roll Book, Alphabetical Admissions Register, 1890-1908*, in possession of ex-Captain E. J. Berkelmans. The discrepancies between the two columns may result from part-time workers, such as shopboys, paperboys, houseboys, and so on, being classified as 'schoolboys' in the second column. Nevertheless, since these are the only pre-1914 figures for any company in Enfield to have survived, it was felt to be worthwhile to tabulate them here.

28.   Dr Leslie Ridge, '1st Enfield B.B. Co.' in *The Enfield Battalion Souvenir Handbook, 1888-1948* (Enfield, 1948), p. 2. Alan Ridge's diary refers to a 'free fight', occasioned by a 'row outside', when Captain Harry Toms 'knocked out a hooligan!' Cf. *Extracts from a diary of events, 1889-1893*, enc. in letter of A. J. Ridge to R. L. Ridge, 17 February 1943; in the possession of E. J. Berkelmans.

29.   Cited in interview with Dr Ben Ridge, 28 August 1974, Enfield.

30.   In the post-Second World War period, some 95 per cent of Boys' Brigade officers graduated from the ranks. See *The Haynes Report on the Work and Future of the Boys' Brigade*, Brigade Headquarters, Feb. 1964, p. 21.

31.   See P. B. Nevill, *Scouting in London, 1908-1965* (London, 1966), pp. 169-172; J. M. Napier, *Some Notes on the History of the Scout Movement in London* (London Scout Council, 1951), pp. 4-5.

32.   See Anon., 'Past and Present: a review of the Enfield Scout Groups' in *Enfield Boy Scouts, 1957 Jubilee Year Book* (Enfield, 1957), p. 20.

33.   'Six Lads saw the Curate, and Enfield Scouting Began' in the *Enfield Gazette*, 10 May 1957.

34.   See ' "I'm proud of them all", says the old S.-M., Revd A. R. Browne (78) meets his Scouts of 40 years ago' in *Enfield Weekly Herald*, 2 May 1952.

35.   Called a Junior Cadet Corps, their rather bizarre uniform consisted of very long 'shorts', jerseys, Scout hats and Eton collars. The 1st Enfield Troop suffered from a lack of Scoutmasters after the First World War; and even

after the formation of a Rover Crew in 1919, it was still being run largely
by Patrol Leaders. It became more stabilized in the 1930s through registration with the London Diocesan Boy Scouts Association.

36.   Viz., the 1st (later 2nd Enfield Methodist) North Enfield, formed 1909,
based on St Michael's Anglican Church at Gordon Hill; the 1st (later 3rd
Enfield) Ponders End Troop, 1909-1918, based on the Congregational
Church Hall in Hertford Road, Enfield; and the 4th Enfield (St Andrew's)
formed in 1911, affiliated to an Anglican Church but using the Old Mission
Hall in Baker Street, Enfield, for its Headquarters.

37.   I am grateful to the late P. B. Nevill for permission to utilize the documentary collection on this troop in his possession. Henceforward prefixed:
Nevill Papers, A-G, files, 1-20.

38.   Percy Bantock Nevill (1887-1975). See Biographical Notes.

39.   P. B. Nevill, *My Scouting Story*, (London, 1960), p. 11.

40.   *Notes of a speech by Nevill inaugurating the 5th. Enfield*, 2 October 1909,
at St. Paul's Church, holograph Ms., Nevill Papers, G. 11.

41.   Ian Niall, *A London Boyhood* (London, 1974), p. 115. Cf. Revd H. S.
Pelham, *The Training of a Working Boy* (London, 1914), p. 121; Jerrold
W. Law, 'Scouting and the Workhouse Boy' in *The Headquarters Gazette*,
14 November 1911, p. 23.

42.   See A. J. Taylor, 'The Economy' in Simon Nowell-Smith (ed.), *Edwardian
England* (London, 1964), pp. 106-138; E. H. Phelps Brown, *The Growth of
British Industrial Relations: a study from the standpoint of 1906-1914*
(London, 1965 edn.), chap. 1; A. R. Prest, *Consumers' Expenditure in the
United Kingdom, 1900-1919* (London, 1954); Peter Wilsher, *The Pound in
Your Pocket 1870-1970* (London, 1970), p. 94.

43.   Scout Harrington to Nevill, 22 July 1910, (original spelling), Nevill Papers,
B. 3; Scout Oddy of Cecil Ave., Enfield, wrote to Nevill: 'being out of work
some time I want to know if I can obtain permission to leave the Scouts
until I get more work'. Another anonymous Boy Scout scribbled a pencilled note on 6 April 1910 demanding: 'would you let me have that 2/4d.
that I gave you as my mother thinks I had better not continue in the
Scouts.' Nevill Papers, A.1, B.1.

44.   The 5th Enfield was originally formed at St Paul's Presbyterian (now
United Reform) Church; it started in 1906, as an 'open' Troop, then, in
July 1911, moved to Bush Hill Park, where it used a corrugated iron hut,
known locally as the 'Iron Room'; the hut was the original St Mark's
Church building and has since been demolished.

45.   Boy Scouts from the socially 'respectable' area of Bush Hill Park more often
became Patrol Leaders and, given an annual turnover of at least a dozen
boys, were more likely to stay in the Troop over a period of years rather
than months, viz., Patrol Leader Chadwick, son of a Sub-Inspector of
Schools, from West Brae, Wellington Road; Scout Beaven, son of a wholesale family grocer and licensee in London Road; Troop Leader Dimmock,
son of a 'Professor' of Music, who ran the local silver prize band, living in
middle-class Southbury Road, Enfield, Evidence for a proper social analysis
of this troop was not available.

46.   See accounts of the Middlesex Rally from pencilled reports of Boy Scouts,
Nevill Papers, G. 14. On 5th Enfield Camps, see *infra*, chap. 6.

47.   See Nevill, *My Scouting Story*, p. 45. The University Camps for Public
Schoolboys movement was founded in 1892 by Major Seton Churchill.

48.   Frederick Haydn Dimmock, *Bare Knee Days* (London, 1937), p. 25; the
addresses given for the Assistant Scoutmasters of the Troop also suggest
middle-class elegance viz., Chase Green Avenue, Stamford Hill, Carlton

Mansion, River View, Hill Lodge, Clay Hill.

49. For a list of the Troop's weekly activities see Nevill, p. 31. In April 1910, as part of their Second Class Badge Test Answers, the 5th were asked to write a short account of the most enjoyable way of spending an evening in the Club Room. See Nevill Papers, D. 4, 6, 7.

50. On taking their Second Class Badge Tests, Boy Scouts were asked to perform such tasks as: drawing the Union Jack, writing out Baden-Powell's name in semaphore, defining a Good Turn, and writing out the Scout's Promise, as well as explaining why it is that a Scout does not smoke ('it stunts the growth, encourages spitting and also encourages laziness.') See *Questions and Answers, April 1910, Second Class Badge Tests,* Nevill papers, D. 11, 12, 14.

51. The 5th were entertaining a band of Norwegian Boy Scouts and had to spend some time in arranging the safe return of their guests. See Nevill, pp. 39-40.

52. See Nevill, *Memoranda re. Scouts on duty at the Royal Small Arms Factory,* Boys Scout Assoc., Enfield District, marked: 'copies of memos, issued in connection with Lady Lawrence's Night Canteen at the Enfield Lock Small Arms Factory where Scouts assisted from the start, to the closing of the concern, a period of nine months.' Nevill Papers; cf. Haydn Dimmock, pp. 45-46; Nevill, pp. 41-42.

53. Viz., Scout Stanley Eastwick, a station porter in Enfield, became a ship's stoker and was killed in the Battle of Jutland on 31 May 1916; Patrol Leader Evans was also killed in the Navy; Patrol Leader R. M. Purnell was killed when the Scout ketch *Mirror* was accidentally run doen off Gravesend in 1913; Patrol Leader George Ison became a stretcher-bearer and was killed during one of the Somme offensives; Patrol Leader W. H. Hart was killed accidentally in 1917 while working as an air-mechanic. Sources: obituaries in the *Enfield Observer:* Eastwick, 19 December 1916; Purnell, 31 October 1913; Ison, 27 October 1916; Hart, 9 February 1917. Cf. Private George Ison to P. B. Nevill, 16 September 1916, pencil Ms., Log Book, Nevill Papers.

6 SUMMER CAMP

To attempt a history of British youth movements without mentioning
the subject of camping would be rather like writing a history of nineteenth century China without mentioning opium. For to most boys
who joined an organized youth movement, camping was by far the
greatest attraction it could offer:

> Ask any recruit when he joins his Company what he is looking
> forward to most and he will reply — Camp, [a Boys' Brigade Captain
> declared] talk to any 'Old Boy' about his experiences while a
> member of the Brigade, and the conversation will most certainly
> turn to Camp — yes, the word 'camp' is magic — it just sets one
> talking and talking.[1]

Without a doubt, a week or more spent under canvas was *the* major
event of the year, dreamt about expectantly for months beforehand.
Camp represented liberation from the restraints of school and family,
the noise and dirt of urban existence, the unimaginativeness and urban
squalor which was the setting of the lives of so many boys from the
industrial conurbations.[2] Above all, it offered the potential of excitement and adventure: a model of a fuller, more active and satisfying
existence. Camp was a safety valve for the frustrated energies of boys
confined for most of the year to the city streets for their entertainment
and relaxation.

It is rare for accounts of camp written by their participants to have
survived, except for those reports written by adult leaders for their
own official publications. By and large, the documentary evidence
offers the point of view of authority, whose tone in describing the
camping experience ranges from the arch to the lyrical, from the
moralistic to the patronising. Yet reading between the lines, there is
no denying the profound impact of a summer camp by the sea-side on
the boys' consciousness:

> There can be no question of the vast benefit such a week's outing
> confers on London working boys, [wrote Major Salmond in command
> of the Southwark Cadet Battalion at camp near Churn, Berkshire]
> the change of scene, fresh air, good food, regular discipline, and

prompt attention to duties produce invaluable results.[3]

One ex-Scoutmaster more recently remembered camping as a test of
the boys' self-reliance:

> The point when the boy thinks: 'I'm away from all the schooling, all
> the 'telly, all the other, all the motor cars — and I'm surviving,
> survival of the fittest, I've got a bit of grub and if I want some more
> I'll have to go and find it or 'ave a walk down the road three miles
> or something, 'cause I 'aven't used me nut an' brought enough with
> me'. They want to get away from the other for a while — they begin
> to appreciate the countryside.[4]

From the rather condescending point of view of the adult leader in the
Boys' Brigade, with his elevated social background in relation to his boy
charges, the countryside was more often seen as offering a physical
means of escape from the much despised life of the industrial cities.
One officer wrote in 1903:

> We with our fair conditions of life at home and school do not
> realize even one little bit what the poor lads of our busy manu-
> facturing town have to live amongst and endure . . . the Boys' Brigade,
> its drill and festivities, and more than all, its annual camp, is indeed
> a boon and a blessing — a bright star in their lives pointing to so
> much that is higher and nobler than anything else around them.[5]

Another observed: 'the Boys from the smoke and hard streets of the
city rejoiced at the lovely scenery and the soft carpet of grass on which
they were to live for the next four days.'[6] In 1902 the Secretary of
the Bristol Battalion of the Boys' Brigade wrote a eulogistic piece 'In
Praise of Camp', which represents the apogee of the laudatory approach
to outdoor life:

> Who has really felt the majesty of the starlit sky, [he pondered] who
> has not stepped from a lighted tent into the hush of a midnight
> camp, his face fanned by the gentle zephyrs blowing in from the sea,
> whose murmur makes the blessed silence yet more still! Who but has
> heard the gentle tap, tap, of a passing shower on the canvas over his
> sleepless head knows the true mystery and magic of the rain![7]

The reality for those under canvas was, of course, often somewhat

different from what this idealized paeon of praise to the open air
suggests. A boy in the 76th London Company of the Boys' Brigade
gave a more prosaic account of his own experience of the weather in
camp:

> We had it rather wet during the week, and when I woke up in the
> morning I found that I was lying in a pool of water instead of on
> my mattress. My bed was soaked through, and so was I.[8]

No lyrical expression of being at one with a benevolent Nature in this
statement. Accounts could be multiplied of boys being washed from
their tents by torrents of rain, eventually to be sent home, the camp
abandoned. In 1903, for example, one camp near Weymouth was
drenched during the wettest week of the wettest June then on record,
'our tents were soaked, the mess tent was a quagmire, the wind blew a
hurricane, and the rain descended in torrents the whole day.'[9] Undeter-
red by the harsher realities of camp life, the author of 'In Praise of Camp'
went on to describe the pleasures of early rising:

> Only to dwellers in tents is the real sweetness of early morning
> brought home — the grass heavy with glistening dew, the golden
> radiance of the level sunshine illuminating the white mantle of mist,
> the delicious coldness of a morning plunge! These things are the
> poetry of camp, and not the least of its joys to some of us.[10]

A more disenchanted, down-to-earth account of waking up in the
morning during a weekend Scout camp in the 1920s, is given by Ian
Niall drawing upon memories of his own childhood:

> By morning all glamour had gone. A fire of greenwood refused to
> heat our pots but poured a heavy grey smoke into the tent. No one
> wanted to go out in the drizzle, so we sat and suffocated in the tent.
> Our Scoutmaster, who had taken himself home to a comfortable bed
> for the night, arrived about the time when we whould have been
> preparing our mid-day meal although we hadn't had our breakfast.[11]

Another side to camping, of declining importance, is that of social
conditioning: training the boys in middle-class manners and patterns of
behaviour generally:

> Then what a grand place is a camp to teach tidiness! Why the whole

thing gives an object lesson! [exclaimed the President of the Carlisle
Battalion of the Boys' Brigade] Where possible grace should be
said. Boys should be taught manners, such as eating with their
mouths shut, not seizing the best pieces; here again priceless lessons
can be given by a watchful officer.[12]

Other officers put less emphasis on strict military discipline and more on
the Evangelical religious potential of a camp. The owner of a field placed
at the disposal of the Boys' Brigade expected every boy in the camp to
attend an Evangelistic meeting held at his house one Sunday evening.[13]
Drumhead services, Church parades and prayers were a common feature
of a Boys' Brigade camp. 'Young, manly Christian men' pictured as
being in an ideal situation to convert impressionable boys, were 'one of
the most potent factors in the Christianisation of a certain stratum of
society before which so many other agencies are either indifferent or
impotent.'[14] There is little evidence, however, of similar forms of
indoctrination being attempted in the Boy Scouts; although this would
depend on the personality of the individual Scoutmaster in charge of
the camp.

In general, Scout camps appear from contemporary testimony to
have been less organized, more flexible and spontaneous than their
Boys' Brigade counterparts. They could, of course, dispense with the
strict necessities of religious supervision and military discipline demanded of the Boys' Brigade and the Church Lads' Brigade. In fact, only
the saluting of the Union Jack after breakfast appears to have been
taken wholly seriously in many Boy Scout camps. For, as a 1950
survey of youth organizations in Birmingham pointed out:

The typical Brigade camp is large and highly organized, with all
the tents pitched with military precision, while the typical Scout
camp is an expedition in which a patrol of half a dozen boys adventure
forth on their own.[15]

Discipline in a Boys' Brigade camp was run strictly along military lines,
as the stern-sounding Standing Orders of the 1890s amply demonstrate.[16]
The typical Scout camp was more relaxed and less well organized,
lacking in military precision and a sense of order:

After pulling the goods etc. there we pitched our tents prepared the
camp and then settled down to tea, [writes a Boy Scout of a weekend

camp in 1910] after tea was finished we had a sing song round the
camp fire . . . and then we trooped off to our respective tents to
sleep . . . at half past three we were woke by the noise of the occu-
pants of the other tent which also brought a policeman to see what
all the noise was about.[17]

The Boys' Brigade proceeded more circumspectly, as befitting their
larger numbers:

The Company detrained four miles from camp so that their [boys']
energies might be worked off before night, [reports a prudent officer
in 1901] and with the satisfactory result that 'lights out' was followed
by practically absolute silence. The usual camp routine was followed:
strict discipline and punctuality were enforced, and really appeared to
be appreciated by the Boys.[18]

How did the actual practice of camping differ among Scouts, Brigades
and Cadets, particularly before 1914? In August 1911, Patrol Leader
Evans kept a diary of the 5th Enfield Troop's annual camp held on a
farm near Worthing, which captures the authentic flavour of a Boy
Scout camp: reveille at 6.30 on a Sunday morning, an early morning
bathe spoilt by rocks at low tide, a church service after breakfast,
another 'bathing-parade' at high tide, the rest of the afternoon and early
evening being spent seeing the sights around camp, then cocoa and biscuits before turning in to their tents. They had only one blanket apiece
for, owing to the 1911 railway strike, the other blankets did not arrive
until the following Monday. The only excitement of the camp came
when the Boy Scouts were aroused from their sleep by their first
night attack:

Adj. King whilst on his knees stalking the raiders was seen by P. L.
Riddell, who mistaking Adj. King for the enemy advanced fiercely
brandishing his staff and would have smote him had not somebody
pulled him back.

After the fierce waving of staves and brave speeches, the raiders sur-
rendered and proved to be some Scouts from Worthing who were in
search of a few Union Jacks to decorate their Headquarters as trophies
of their skill in camp raiding. 'When the raid was nearly over P. L. Hart
appeared on the scene with hopes of a fight and seemed angry when he
found that the raiders were Scouts and not "Roughs".'[19] The perennial

Scout fear of 'roughs' or tramps invading the sacred acres of their camp site, evokes a sense of a barbaric and violent underworld waiting to take over from the comfortable world of the Edwardian privileged. A few days later the narrator records:

> A few men who looked like tramps were seen hanging about the camp all day and so at night special care was taken by the guards, one of the men attempted to get to the stores after Lights Out but he made himself scarce at the sight of Adj. King, two guards slept in the store tent all night.[20]

The usual routine of a typical day in a Boys' Brigade camp would start with reveille at 6 a.m.; at least before 1914 this would be the practice. After breakfast at 7.30 came morning prayers, the hearty singing of the boys often being led by a quartette of the band. Camp inspection came next, after the 'fatigue squad' had done their work, and this was usually followed by a route march with the band at its head. The 1st Glasgow Company at camp in the Kyles of Bute would then go out in four-oared boats to pull across to the bathing place. After dinner the boys were usually free to roam over the hills surrounding the camp alongside the Loch, to play cricket, or to visit the nearby small resorts of Portavadie and Tighnabruaich in Argyll. It was near here at Auchen-lochan that the first ever Boys'Brigade camp was held in 1886 during Glasgow Fairs Week. After tea there might be a fishing parade in the camp boats, the long eventful day usually closing with a supper of cocoa and biscuits, evening prayers and 'Lights Out' at 10.30.[21] By contrast, at the first Jewish Lads' Brigade Camp at Deal, Kent, in 1897, the routine was slightly different: for at 6.30 morning prayers, 'all but one lad came down duly provided with his Tephillin and everyone without exception displays his Arbang Confes.'[22] Some of the boys who went for an early morning bathe had never even seen the sea before, while the majority had only spent a day at Clacton. Physical drill was followed by breakfast; then the boys 'brailled-up' their sleeping tents and generally tidied up the camp: this was followed by an hour of rifle drill. Basically, the morning was for work and the rest of the day for play, including cricket and chess. All the meals were strictly 'kosher'. Games continued until a little before supper at 9.00, and 'Lights Out' were at 10.15.[23]

The numbers present at the 1st London Cadet Battalion's annual camps in the 1890s rarely exceeded 150, owing to each boy having to contribute five shillings to camp expenses and, in addition, forfeit a

week's wages. As might be expected, their routine was more conspicuous for military drill and discipline than that of any other youth
movement. Reveille was sounded as early as 5.45 in the morning,
parade followed at 7.00 (if the grass was not too wet), then breakfast
at 8.00, orderly room at 9.00, drill parade at 9.30, dinner at 1.00,
parade again at 2.30 in the afternoon, and tea at 5.00. All boys had to
be back in camp at 10.00 and 'Lights Out' was at 10.30. Anyone caught
talking after 'Lights Out' was sent to the Guard Room for the night and
sentenced to punishment drill at the Orderly Room next morning. A
guard was kept on duty all day and night which, curiously enough,
was amongst the most popular of the cadet's duties. 'All night long our
little sentries paced up and down,' observed one officer, 'only too
delighted if they could see anyone to challenge.'[24]

The actual content of Boys' Brigade camps can be made subject to
analysis, based on the detailed reports of both company and battalion
annual camps sent in by the officers in command to the *Boys' Brigade
Gazette* under the heading of 'Camp Notes'. Table 1 covers over 150
such reports printed in 'Camp Notes' during a four year sample period.
It gives an indication of the general categories into which the more than
700 individual items mentioned can be said to fall. The 'miscellaneous'
category is so prominent because it includes items like the weather
(Table 2) and eating arrangements, which were of central concern to
the campers. Even so, the range of activities described in these 'Camp
Notes' is by no means all-inclusive. For, if an attempt is made to break
down the general categories of events into a more precise ranking order
based on the frequency of reference to individual items (Table 3),
how else to account for the low itemization of such obviously popular
activities as football, and such frequently occurring events as church
services? The answer, presumably, is that the nature of these reports
must have put at a minimum the mention of everyday routine events,
such as morning prayers, in favour of the more unique, 'once a year'
occasions, such as the Camp Sports Day. Even this last named event
only rated one reference more than the weather, which suggests that
among criteria of selection for appearance in 'Camp Notes' can be
included either novelty or an event with decisive effect on the camp's
morale.

If the nature of such reports of annual camps does put at a minimum
the mention of everyday routine practices, it nevertheless reflects
reasonably accurately the importance of sporting or boating and
bathing activities, which together account for 22 per cent of the general
categories of events measured and 134 or 38 per cent of the 353 selected

Table 1: General Categories of Events in Camps,
Boys' Brigade, 1901-1904[25]

Type of Event*	1901	1902	1903	1904	Total	%
Miscellaneous	39	42	39	70	190	26
Sports and Games	61	36	21	43	161	22
Special Camp Events	58	26	31	42	157	21
Regular Camp Events	45	24	20	33	122	17
Religion and Services	26	22	14	39	101	14
Totals	229	150	125	227	731	100

* Regular Camp Events = camp inspections, fatigue parties, visitors' day, drills etc.
  Special Camp Events = route-marches, excursions, concerts, bands, picnics, etc.
  Miscellaneous = the weather, local hosts, accommodation, meals, discipline, etc.

Table 2: Types of Weather Experienced in Camps,
Boys' Brigade, 1901-1904[26]

Type	1901	1902	1903	1904	Totals	%
Stormy weather	3	3	2	6	14	30
Wet or unsettled	2	7	5	-	14	30
Camps flooded	-	1	3	1	5	10
Good or hot	5	-	3	6	14	30
Totals	10	11	13	13	47	100

individual items. On the other hand, religion accounts for 77 or 22 per
cent of the most frequently mentioned single items, which is itself an
achievement, considering how much more pressure there must have been
to include the exceptional in one's report to the *Gazette.* From such a
breakdown, however, doubts might be cast upon the assumption, often
canvassed among employers, that Boys' Brigade camps were exclusively

Table 3: Most Popular Single Camp Activities, Boys' Brigade
1901-1904[27]

Camp Activity*	1901	1902	1903	1904	Totals	%
Camp Sports Day	16	10	6	16	48	14
Boating/Bathing	14	10	5	10	39	11
Church Parades	6	11	2	13	32	9
Camp Inspections	13	6	4	9	32	9
Visitors' Day	12	7	5	7	31	9
Cricket	14	4	4	5	27	8
Excursions/Visits	13	1	8	5	27	8
Route-Marches	10	5	4	7	26	7
Camp Concerts	11	5	2	8	26	7
Drumhead Services	8	6	4	5	23	6
Church Services	9	1	4	8	22	6
Football	13	2	2	3	20	6
Totals	139	68	50	96	353	100

* No activity has been included in this table with less than twenty references.

centres of drill, discipline and religion. Curiously, in 1901 one of the
Presidents of a Brigade Battalion performed a similar exercise by
analysing one month's camp reports in the *Gazette* and dividing them
up under the two headings of 'Recreation' and 'Education'. He con-
cluded that 'Recreation' was much the larger group and that equal
care should be put into 'arranging for the supply of instruction that
we exhibit in providing amusement.'[28]

From the employer's point of view, the annual camp meant the
absence of some of his cheap boy-labour for a week or more, which
may explain the element of special pleading evident in Church Lads'
Brigade editorials:

We hope that employers of our lads will read the accounts [of
camp] given in this number, [reads a typical example] and we
believe, to hear of the happy time they have had and of the good
behaviour, will be of some small reward to them for the inconvenience they have been put to in giving their lads a holiday.[29]

But altruism was not the only motive the Brigade appealed to, for it
was also suggested that the camps instilled habits which would make
the boys better employees for the experience:

> We are confident that the sacrifices they [the employers] have
> made will be made up to them by the better service which the
> lads will render during the year, from the habits of order and
> discipline, and the new stock of health they will have acquired.[30]

To the parents, some of whom came to the camp site on Visitors' Day
taking advantage of the special cheap fares many of the railway companies provided[31] — there may have been the added satisfaction of
seeing their sons trained in public-school manliness, thrift and self-
reliance. Together with the strict military organization necessary for
discipline in the Brigades, camping:

> fitted the lads to be better citizens in the future by making them,
> in the present, discharge their daily duties to their employers
> better by means of the habits they have learnt in the Camps.[32]

Most past and present members of a youth movement will have little
difficulty in recalling amusing or memorable incidents that have occurred to them while at camp. Everyone has his or her favourites, such as:

> The year the entire paraffin supply went up in flames, the year of
> gales and storms when tents collapsed and frying pans took flight in
> the kitchen tent, the year it rained incessantly and the only way
> round the camp site was on duck boards, and morale was difficult
> to maintain in the face of mud and persistent damp, the year a
> first year boy brought home a catch of fish for his mother in the
> coach.[33]

In general, taking their cue from the Ralph Reader Gang Shows, to most
outsiders the traditional sing-songs around the camp-fire act as a convenient symbol for Scouting activities. Even the Scout himself, looking
back from the vantage point of maturity, conveniently forgets much of
the actual discomfort involved in camping: the rainy weather, long
journeys and often unappetizing food. It would not be difficult to cite
a more jaundiced version of camping from the point of view of the
contemporary Boy Scout, especially if he was a Patrol Leader obliged
to do all the work of cooking and clearing away meals.[34] Yet, while
the realities of rainy weather and tents being flooded out act as a useful

corrective to the generally glowing versions more often given of camping, they are not necessarily any more representative of the average
boys' experience. Reminiscences of the annual camp also suggest that
how the past is perceived through nostalgia can often be as important
to the narrator as what actually happened. Ultimately, camping
provided a pastoral frame of moral reference for British youth
movements.

Notes

1.   A. D. Wiltshire, 'Camp and Camping' in Anon., *The Enfield Battalion
      Souvenir Handbook, 1888-1948* (Enfield, 1948), p. 12.
2.   Encapsulated by this lament on the return home from a Scout Camp:
      'Back to London, back to work/Back to houses, back to dirt/Dirt in all
      the streets and skies/Dirt that makes you rub your eyes.' Cited in
      'Extracts from the Little Baddow Buster', August 1910, *5th Enfield
      Camp Magazine*, P. B. Nevill Log Book, Reigate, Surrey.
3.   Albert L. Salmond, *Report for 1893*, 1st Cadet Battalion, 'the Queen's',
      Royal West Surrey Regiment, p. 4. Archives of Hoare's Bank, Fleet Street,
      London.
4.   Extract from taped interview with G. G. Wilkinson, ex-Scoutmaster, 2nd
      Edmonton Troop. Recorded 2 January 1973, Edmonton, London.
5.   A. Hume Smith, 'A Company Camp' in *The Boys' Brigade Gazette*,
      Vol. XII, 2 March 1903, p. 102.
6.   Aberdeen 'Camp Notes', ibid., 1 September 1903, p. 5.
7.   J. Harold Price, 'In Praise of Camp', ibid., 1 March 1902, p. 109.
8.   Anon., 'My Experiences at Camp' in *The Brigadier*, Vol. III, No. 1
      (Oct., 1903), p. 8.
9.   Yeovil and District 'Camp Notes' in *The Boys' Brigade Gazette*, Vol. XII,
      1 September 1903, p. 11. Cf. 'Late in the afternoon, our C.O. ordered the
      camp to Weymouth and the Boys reposed for the night upon the floors of
      the schoolroom of the Gloucester St Church, rolled in their blankets.' Ibid.
10.   Harold Price, *Gazette*.
11.   Ian Niall, *A London Boyhood* (London, 1974), pp. 118-119.
12.   F. R. M'Connel, 'Camps, Company and Battalion' in *The Boys' Brigade
      Gazette*, Vol. X, 1 November 1901, p. 43. He also says:

      We must think of what many of the poor little chaps are accustomed
      to at home. Think how some have never been taught to be tidy, to fold
      or brush their clothes, to behave at meals like civilised beings, or even
      to wash properly. If our camps taught them these things only, they
      would be well worth having. But *do* we pay enough attention to these?

13.   Cork 'Camp Notes', ibid., 1 September 1903, p. 7.
14.   Revd Edward W. Lewis, 'A Battalion Camp', ibid., 1 September 1902, p. 14.
15.   Anon., *Eighty Thousand Adolescents: a study of young people in the city
      of Birmingham by the staff and students of Westhill Training College*
      (London, 1950), p. 93.
16.   West Kent District Boys' Brigade, *Camp Regulations, 1895-1899, Standing*

Orders, Foolscap Notebook, 1st Blackheath (Kent), Company Records; Boys' Brigade Archives, London.

17. Boy Scout C. Evans, 5th Enfield (Bush Hill Park) Troop, 'Description of a Weekend Camp', June 1910, Nevill Papers, Reigate, Surrey.
18. Colchester 'Camp Notes' in *The Boys' Brigade Gazette*, Vol. X, No. 1, 2 September 1901, p. 7.
19. Patrol Leader C. Evans, 'Camp 1911', Nevill Papers. Adj. = Adjutant, a rank later dropped; P.L. = Patrol Leader.
20. *Loc. cit.*
21. See 1st Glasgow Co., 'Camp Notes' in *The Boys' Brigade Gazette*, Vol. XII, 1 September 1903, p. 5. In July 1972, together with a colleague, the author made a pilgrimage to the site of the first Boys' Brigade Camp, taking a car ferry to the Kyles from Gourock.
22. Anon., 'A Visit to the Jewish Lads' Brigade Seaside Camp', leaflet on 'The Jewish Lads' Brigade' reprinted from the *Jewish Chronicle* (1897?), p. 8. Mocatta Library, University College, London. Tephillin = phylacteries donned during morning prayer; Arbang Confes (arba kanfes) = a fringed garment worn at morning service.
23. Ibid., pp. 8-9.
24. W. Ingham Brooke, 'Our Camp at Churn', leaflet, reprinted from *The Charity Organization Review*, p. 4. Archives, Hoare's Bank.
25. Taken from 'Camp Notes', *The Boys' Brigade Gazette*, Vol. X, No. 1, 2 September 1901 to Vol. XIII, No. 2, 1 October 1904.
26. Ibid.
27. Ibid.
28. F. R. M'Connell, *Gazette*, p. 44.
29. Editorial, '1898 Camps' in *The Brigade*, Vol. IV, No. 10 (October 1898), p. 211.
30. *Loc. cit.*
31. See Aberdeen 'Camp Notes' in the *Boys' Brigade Gazette*, 1 September 1904, p. 5. During the three days this camp was open to visitors, 2,800 parents paid for admission and 200 came by invitation of the officers.
32. Editorial, *The Brigade*, p. 210.
33. Anon., (Ursula Mason), *Men and Brothers: the story of a Boys' Brigade Company, 2nd. West Kent (Blackheath) Co., 1893-1968* (London, 1969), p. 25.
34. Cf. 'B . . . . . Prepared. John Hall on the problems of putting a dozen young-sters on stage in a play about God, Queen and Country', the *Guardian*, 8 September 1972, p. 10; inc. interview with 'Big Del' of Feltham Comprehensive who appeared in Jonothan Hales' play *Brussel Sprouts* at the Royal Court Theatre Upstairs in October 1972.

7 GREEN JERKINS AND BACK-TO-NATURE

Co-educational, non-religious and non-military, the English woodcraft groups of the 1920s were all, to some degree, off-shoots of the more sober and down-to-earth Scout movement with which, despite appearances, they shared many basic attributes. During the First World War, the enthusiastic support given to the military authorities by Baden-Powell disenchanted several of his more internationalist, pacifist Scoutmasters. It was as a result of their critical stand that the woodcraft groups considered here emerged: the Order of Woodcraft Chivalry in 1916, Kibbo Kift Kindred in 1920 and the Woodcraft Folk in 1925. In reaction against orthodox Scouting methods with, for the Left, their imperialist and militarist associations, the woodcraft groups claimed to offer a viable alternative combining naturalism with socialism:

> We should recognize once and for all [exclaimed one such rebel Scout leader] that the ideas and ideals which may have fitted fairly well into the social fabric of 1908 may be very ill-fitting 'reach-me-downs' in 1920.[1]

What actually did the small woodcraft groups try to put in place of the more established Scout movement's supposedly antiquated values, and why did they meet with so little relative success during the inter-war period?

In 1915 several leading members of Scouting in the Cambridge area broke away from the movement and looked for help to establish an organization which could oppose the military inclinations of the Scouts. They found their leader in Ernest Westlake,[2] the natural scientist, and his son, Aubrey, who had been a Scoutmaster while reading medicine as an undergraduate at Cambridge. With the support of an impressive advisory committee, including several eminent educationalists, they set up the first group of the Order of Woodcraft Chivalry in 1916. Westlake modelled the new Order upon Ernest Thompson Seton's Woodcraft Indians of America (1902), for although all three woodcraft groups were directly or indirectly breakaways from the Boy Scouts, the inspirational influence of Thompson Seton[3] on their outlook was always greater than that of Baden-Powell. Seton's

ideas, methods and the organization he founded were followed very
closely by all the English woodcraft groups.

Developing an interest in evolutionary theory through his scientific
work in geology and anthropology, Ernest Westlake also became
interested in the American social Darwinist G. Stanley Hall's theory of
'recapitulation', which attempted to apply Darwinian biological ideas to
the educational psychology of adolescence.[4] Basically, Stanley Hall
argued that every developing adolescent 'recapitulated' the cultural
history of the human race in the stages of his or her own physical and
mental development. This idea held a special attraction for the woodcraft groups in that it provided for a scheme of youth training based on
the belief that the child has to live through all the stages of mankind
before he can appreciate and accept the present stage of evolution.
It offered a justification for the pursuit of the tribal and primitive
which these movements so conspicuously displayed.

The first recorded attempt to implement the ideas of the Order of
Woodcraft Chivalry was made at Sidcot Lodge, the famous Quaker
Secondary School in Somerset, in the summer of 1916. This was
followed by a test of its methods with a group of slum children in the
East End of London and at a camp for Belgian refugee children in
Northern France, run by the Friends' War Victims Relief Committee.[5]
The programme for Ernest Westlake's advanced educational techniques,
as outlined in his *The Forest School or Evolutionary Education,* appeared
in parts between 1917 and 1925. The basic aim was to give the child an
opportunity to 'recapitulate' the ancestral and racial experience by
passing through the various stages of man's evolution: in the form of
colourful ritual, ceremonial and woodcraft training, which contained
elements from both the Boy Scouts and Seton's Woodcraft Indians.
The Order of Woodcraft Chivalry was governed by an elected National
Council of Guidance under the British Chieftain, and local groups
called Lodges were in turn grouped into Guilds. In 1923 Ernest Thompson
Seton was made honorary Grand Chieftain but most of the organization
of the Order was in the hands of Aubrey Westlake who, after the
tragic death of his father in a car accident in 1922, held the post of
Marshal. Even before Ernest Westlake's death, there had been a serious
split between those members of the National Council of Guidance who
represented the National Sunday School, mission and settlement
organizations, and those who, supporting Stanley Hall's 'recapitulation'
theories, wanted an English woodcraft movement along the lines of
Seton's Woodcraft Indians.[6]

The Order of Woodcraft Chivalry typified more the reaction of a small group of middle-class intellectuals to the mechanized, urban-industrial life which they explicitly rejected rather than a popular working-class or socialist alternative to the Boy Scouts. From the educational standpoint, their child-centred theory was loosely in the tradition of Rousseau's novel *Emile*, while the element of pantheist nature worship in their ceremonies places them firmly in the early-nineteenth century romantic tradition of antipathy to capitalist industrial society. The appeal of the Order was based less on practical politics than a utopian search for individual freedom through the open-air life of poetry, adventure and play. It attempted to cultivate a sense of beauty and harmony in its members by the use of colour, dancing, symbolism and ceremony. Yet despite the intellectual energies of its founders, the Order never really developed into anything other than a small (in the 1930s around 220), middle-class, family-centred, largely Quaker group, with a strong poetic, individualist tone that did not help to expand its numbers.[7] After the Second World War, only a few families of OWC supporters remained but they continued to hold their picturesque annual ceremonies at the attractive national head-quarters of Sandyballs, Godshill, in the New Forest. Today the OWC still survives with a membership of around 300, preserving its character as an elite woodcraft movement and maintaining an extremely high standard of training, but offering little competition to the major youth movements.

In 1919 the leaders of the OWC came into contact with John Hargrave,[8] a man of powerful personal magnetism, who had served as a stretcher-bearer at Gallipoli, and was at this time Commissioner for Camping and Woodcraft at Scout Headquarters. But although Hargrave's name appears on the Order's Council of Guidance, he does not appear to have taken any active part in their leadership.[9] Hargrave was also — together with Clement Attlee, then Mayor of Stepney — on the Committee of the Camelot Club in Poplar, which attempted to promote socialism and internationalism, while working within the mainstream Scouting movement.[10] The strains of working to change the management of Scouting from within must have begun to tell on Hargrave's rather impatient, egocentric personality. For in 1920 he began to write a series of provocative articles as the spokesman of a woodcraft-Left revolt against what he believed to be the established Scout leadership's militarist and imperialist tendencies.[11] The reaction of the London Scout Council to this self-evident display of 'disloyalty' was, by a vote of 39 to 30, on 24 January 1921, to prevent Hargrave from writing in any Scout magazine or from speaking at any Scout meeting and to cancel his warrant as a Commissioner.[12]

Hargrave's attitude to the identification of Scouting with the war effort was shared by other Scoutmasters in London who joined with him in the launching of a new movement – Kibbo Kift, the Wood-craft Kindred, already formally established in August 1920; the name being archaic English for 'Proof of Great Strength'.[13] Although many South London Scoutmasters backed Hargrave in this new venture, the vast majority of the movement remained loyal to Baden-Powell's successfully legitimated leadership. Kibbo Kift placed greater stress on the woodcraft, primitivist, tribal side of Scouting that Hargrave had discovered in Ernest Thompson Seton's writing. The Head Man also borrowed from Stanley Hall's 'recapitulation' theory and was greatly influenced by the utopian world-brotherhood visions of H. G. Wells, characteristic of his writing in the early 1920s.[14] From Wells too came the conception of a New Samurai which gave the Kibbo Kift its uneasy amalgam of elitist leadership with youthful rebelliousness. The inter-nationalist, pacifist and Wellsian ingredients of Kibbo Kift are clearly present in its Covenant, drawn up in the summer of 1920 at meetings held in the Pethick-Lawrences' home in Lincolns Inn Fields, which led to the setting up of the movement.[15] But in the ambivalence of Wellsian socialism lay the possibility of accepting the vague and utopian declarations of the Covenant while retaining the features which made Kibbo Kift a potentially crypto-fascist movement by the 1930s.

Despite receiving support from socialist and Co-operative groups in London, the Kibbo Kift did not prove to be the long-awaited 'Labour Youth Movement'. This failure was as much a result of personality clashes as of ideology. Hargrave, 'tall, with sharp, almost Romany features, an acquiline nose, and a mass of wavy black hair,'[16] was undoubtedly a charismatic figure to his followers. One consequence of the increasingly exclusive, secretive and authoritarian trend in his nature was the development of a private language of occult symbolism, as elaborated in his *The Confession of Kibbo Kift* in 1927. Another was that Hargrave's personal, autocratic rule of the Kibbo Kift, com-bined with its élitist doctrines, was soon to lead to a break with the more robustly democratic, Co-operative elements in the organization he had founded. Then, in the late 1920s, Hargrave became a convert to Major Douglas's Social Credit theory and those who wished to remain in the Kindred had to accept their leader's ardent espousal of the 'New Economics'.[17] By the early 1930s, Kibbo Kift had become assimilated into the Social Credit movement and then into the Greenshirts, a militant section of the League of the Unemployed, marking the end of

the Kindred as a youth movement and the beginning of its development
as a political party. In 1935, the Greenshirt Movement for Social Credit
became the Social Credit Party of Great Britain.[18]

Even during the 1920s, the Kibbo Kift was often looked upon by
outsiders as an elitist organization run by 'cranks' and 'faddists'. It was
certainly the most esoteric of all the woodcraft groups set up during
this decade; it was obscured by much pretentious ritual and based on a
muddled philosophy. Their exclusiveness was emphasized by a distinctive costume of variegated colours: a uniform in green or brown,
of Saxon cowl and jerkin, and a Prussian style army cloak, with shorts
and sandals. In 1924, the peak year for the Kindred, the total attendance
at the annual camp was only 236 and by 1931 the number of names in
the 'Kinlog' had fallen as low as 185;[19] figures tiny beside those of the
Scouts or the German youth movements. As the memories of war —
which had initially determined Hargrave's antipathy to orthodox
Scouting methods — faded into the background and the economic
situation showed signs of improvement, the Kin relied increasingly on
the personal magnetism and erratic behaviour of its founder for
internal cohesion. Like Oswald Mosley, with whom he had much in
common, Hargrave was to end up preaching salvation through a form of
economic nationalism. By the 1930s, the romantic tribalism of the
Kibbo Kift had become diverted into the universal panacea of Social
Credit, yet the adoption of Social Credit at least removed the previous
immanentism which had marked the Kibbo Kift outlook.[20]

When the Kibbo Kift was first formed, its novel educational approach
and its internationalist, pacifist and Wellsian declarations had attracted the attention of the progressive Education Committee of the Royal
Arsenal Co-operative Society. Dr C. K. Cullen, a former Scout Commissioner who had met Hargrave in 1919 — while acting as Secretary of
the Camelot Club — persuaded Joseph Reeves, the dedicated socialist
Education Secretary of the RACS, to form several Co-operative tribes
or branches of the Kindred in South London. But despite Co-operative
propaganda and a Kindred camp in Crystal Palace during a Co-
operative demonstration in 1922, very little national support was
forthcoming for a woodcraft auxiliary. Even in the RACS, woodcraft
methods met with a mixed reception from the already well-established
Co-operative Comrades' Circles, a young Co-operators' movement.[21]
It did not help matters that there developed a divergence of opinion
between Co-operative woodcrafters and the rest of the Kibbo Kift
over the basic incompatibility between Hargrave's personal autocratic
regime and the democratic, socialist outlook of the Co-operative

groups. By late 1923, relations between the Co-operative branches and the Kindred were becoming strained and, as a result, the Education Committee of the RACS decided to abandon the formation of more Kibbo Kift tribes, for:

> In the opinion of the Committee, the movement has departed very considerably from its original aims, has discarded the principles of democracy in forms of government, and has become exclusive in the method of recruiting new members.[22]

At the fifth Kibbo Kift 'Althing' or Annual Council, held at High Wycombe in the Whitsun of 1924, Hargrave's leadership came under direct challenge from Co operative South London groups led by Gordon Ellis, a war-time pacifist who later became Education Secretary of the National Union of Teachers. The issue which brought the conflict to the surface was whether or not Hargrave had the power to over-ride the decisions of a local association in dictatorial fashion. The excuse for refusing to recognize the rights of the Co-operative groups was that their putative leader, Leslie Paul,[23] was not yet 18, the qualifying age for adult membership of the Kibbo Kift. As a result of the subsequent withdrawal by this South London Labour and Co-operative section of about one third of the branches, Hargrave irretrievably lost the opportunity of creating a new Left-based, mass alternative to Scouting. After some disarray, during which Leslie Paul, 'a lean, shock-headed young man,'[24] worked briefly with Ellis's group, the basis for a new movement was created: drawing upon the familiar combination of Hall's 'recapitulation' theory, Seton's woodcraft lore and socialist internationalism. Paul believed that if his method of training were proved a success then a new woodcraft group could be founded in close association with the Co-operative movement.

A modest beginning was made on 3 February 1925 when Paul visited the Rushey Green Co-operative Junior Circle of the RACS, and with a clan of only four small boys in Catford started the Wayfarers' Woodcraft Fellowship the following month.[25] Together with a close friend, Sidney Shaw, an unemployed engineer, Paul continued to test his 'tribal training' theories of education for a few months with this small group until a second was formed and they were able to hold a camp together in St Leonard's Forest, near Horsham.[26] Slowly, under Paul's invigorating leadership of a propagandist group of 'inspired young evangelists', the Mossback Lodge, the nucleus of a new movement began to form. Then, on 19 December 1925, four Woodcraft Fellowships held a Folkmoot Conference in the Co-operative Hall at Rye Lane, Peckham, and agreed to form the Woodcraft Folk or Federation of Co-operative Woodcraft Fellowship.[27] The four federated groups, with less than 70 members, all operating within the area of the RACS, drafted a common programme, accepted a Charter and Declaration, and elected Leslie Paul, then only 20, as Headman of the Woodcraft Folk. The name given to this latest attempt at a left-wing youth movement suggests both 'crafters of wood' and an affinity with the German 'volk-ish' movements of the 1920s. Above all, as Paul proclaimed, the Woodcraft Folk was born in the Co-operative movement.[28]

The Woodcraft Folk's programme was a synthesis of 'recapitulation' theory, pacifism, internationalism, socialism and the eugenic ideal, as propounded in the prolific journalism of Leslie Paul.[29] In his *The Folk Trail* (1929), for example, the emphasis is on camp life as an antidote to the evils of industrialism: the pursuit of arts and crafts; tribal organization and training; and the teaching of world history and evolution.[30] Yet the Woodcraft Folk never really reconciled their grandiose ideals of social reconstruction and spiritual regeneration with the more modest aim of training children in woodcraft activities. During the 1920s, demonstrating their Wellsian enthusiasm for internationalism, the Folk were in touch with the German Bünde, the Austrian Red Falcons and the Czech Sokols, as well as being affiliated to Max Winter's Socialist Educational International. Not just another ill-conceived essay at a 'Labour Youth Movement', the Woodcraft Folk proved to be the most resilient and ably led of the woodcraft groups, counting their membership in thousands rather than in hundreds as their nearest rivals did. By avoiding the romantic and exotic excesses of the Kibbo Kift and the obscurantist, sect-like image of the Order of Woodcraft Chivalry, the more working-class oriented Woodcraft Folk grew in numbers until it had an active membership of around 3,000 by the mid-1930s. (Table 1.) But in the 1940s, membership was at a low ebb and recovery was slow during the 1950s after a long period of stagnation. It was not until the 1960s that numbers began to pick up again, eventually overtaking the heights of the 1930s. Today, as an independent auxiliary of the Co-operative education movement, its membership has expanded to about 15,000 organized into Elfins, Pioneers and Venturers, of which about one third are in London and the South East.[31]

Why did the woodcraft groups meet with so little success in the inter-war period, at least in comparison with the mass movements of

Table 1 Total (approx.) Membership Figures for the Woodcraft Folk, 1926-1938[32]

Year	Total membership	Pioneers and Elfins	Kinsfolk (adults)	No. of groups
1926	116			10
1927	270			
1928	341			16
1929	400			25
1930	721			31
1931	780			
1932	1,014			
1933	1,076		349	
1934	1,550			
1935	2,191	1,076	485	72
1936	3,260	2,927	536	
1937	3,518	2,936	582	
1938	4,521	3,748	773	

the Brigades and the Boy Scouts? All the woodcraft groups considered here devised an attractive costume and symbolism, rejected religious orthodoxy and were co-educational, drawing on Stanley Hall's 'recapitulation' theory, Wellsian internationalism and the woodcraft ideas of Ernest Thompson Seton. Clearly, if they criticized the Scout movement for being tied to the intellectual environment of the 1900s, they were equally products of the fashionable non-conformist educational and political ideas of the 1920s. Whereas in the more tolerant 1970s such an outlook has made the Woodcraft Folk increasingly popular, 50 years ago their progressive doctrines only served to discourage many parents of potential members — not to mention the more puritanical sections of the Labour movement in the regions. The meagreness of Co-operative and Labour monetary contributions,[33] also placed the woodcraft groups in a poor relation to their relatively wealthy, well-equipped, nationally-organized rivals, such as the Scouts, who continued to receive large financial donations from industry. On the other hand, the introspective, rather self-enclosed and mutually admiring world of the Order of Woodcraft Chivalry, for example, did not project an image of a group trying to expand — more one of a self-perpetuating, middle-class, family sect. Finally, the militarist-imperialist overtones of much of pre-1914 Scouting gave way in the 1920s to a more streamlined, 'liberal' programme containing much of the appeal of the woodcraft groups but on a level at which the latter could not compete – in the 1930s culminating in the great international jamborees.[34]

'Their idealism kept them independent: their independence kept them small.'[35] Leslie Paul's apophthegm was meant to describe Seton's Woodcraft Indians, but it could be applied with equal validity to the English woodcraft groups. In comparison to the massive assurance of the Scouts and the Boys' Brigade in the inter-war period, the small experimental woodcraft groups remained 'pure' but under-financed, uncompromising but without reliable backers. Their resolutely limited appeal was, to some extent, a result of the failure of the Labour Party, the trades unions and the Co-operative movement to lend their full, unqualified official support to the idea of a left-wing alternative to Scouting. The largely unintentional projection of a 'cranky', middle-class, élitist image also severely restricted the growth of groups ostensibly making their appeal to the children of the essentially conservative working classes. There is little doubt that many more children from working-class homes have, in fact, joined the Boy Scouts in the past rather than woodcraft; for the Scouts have always been a mass movement, rather than a tiny, inward-looking group.

Yet although they have received little attention from the historian, the woodcraft groups, despite their lack of mass-appeal, did constitute a determined attempt to provide a substitute for the Scout movement. They represented an attempt made with skill and professional polish, to bring some of the colour and romantic excitement, as well as the ideological commitment, of the Austrian Red Falcons and other continental youth movements to the — by contrast — staid, uninspired and unimaginative English youth movement scene. In the long run, perhaps, they may even be seen as making a significant contribution to the creation of the so-called 'youth culture' of the post-1945 world. The 'Alternative Society' has more direct links with these small woodcraft groups and their ideals than with the larger, more established youth movements derived primarily from late-nineteenth-century ideals and attitudes.

Notes

1. 'White Fox' (John Hargrave), 'What I'm Driving At', *The Trail* (Nov., 1920), p. 354.
2. Ernest Westlake (1856-1922). See Biographical Notes.
3. Ernest Thompson Seton (1860-1946). See Biographical Notes.
4. An American Professor of Psychology at Harvard, Hall's major work was the two volume *Adolescence*, first published in New York in 1904, which was much influenced by German social-Darwinists and eugenic socialists, such as Karl Pearson in England. See, Paul Wilkinson, 'A Study of Uniformed Youth Movements, 1883-1935', M.A. thesis, 1968, University of Wales, pp. 20-22.
5. Wilkinson, pp. 131-132.
6. Ibid., pp. 132-133.
7. See D. L. Prynn, 'The Socialist Sunday Schools, the Woodcraft Folk and Allied Movements', M.A. thesis, 1971, Sheffield University, Vol. II, pp. 226-242.
8. John Hargrave (1894-   ). See Biographical Notes.
9. See I. O. Evans, *Woodcraft and World Service* (London, 1937), p. 51.
10. See *Camelot Club Report, 1919-1920*, 'Aims and Policy', pp. 2-4, Tower Hamlets Central Library, Local History Section.
11. See Hargrave, 'The Words of White Fox', *The Trail*, Vol. III (Sept., 1920), p. 272, and 'What I'm Driving At', ibid., (Nov., 1920), pp. 353-355; *idem.*, 'The Demilitarization of the Scout Movement', *Foreign Affairs*, Vol. II (Aug., 1920), pp. 26-27. Many of Hargrave's later eclectic tendencies are present in *The Great War Brings It Home* (London, 1919), pp. 51-52.
12. See Annual General Meeting of the London Scout Council, *The Trail*, Vol. IV, No. 37 (Feb., 1921), pp. 49-50.
13. See John Hargrave, *The Confessions of Kibbo Kift* (London, 1927), p. 58; I. O. Evans, p. 64.
14. Particularly influential were: *The Outline of History* (1920) and *Men Like Gods* (1923). In the latter, the hero, Barnstaple, is an ordinary man living in the Age of Confusion who is permitted a glimpse of a happier future when he is carried off to Utopia. See Norman and Jeanne Mackenzie, *The Time Traveller: the life of H. G. Wells* (London, 1973), pp. 336-337.
15. For the Covenant of the Kibbo Kift see: Wilkinson, pp. 159-160; Evans, pp. 64-65.
16. Leslie Paul, *Angry Young Man* (London, 1951), p. 54.
17. See John L. Finlay, *Social Credit: the English Origins* (Montreal, 1972), chap. 7; Social Credit Party, 'A Documented Record of Mr. John Hargrave's Visit to the Province of Alberta, Canada, 1936-1937', pamphlet (London, 1937), Y68, Youth Movement Archive, University College, Cardiff.
18. See J. L. Finlay, 'John Hargrave, the Green Shirts and Social Credit', *The Journal of Contemporary History*, Vol. V, No. 1 (1970), pp. 53-71.
19. Ibid., p. 55.
20. In the late 1920s and 1930s, Aubrey Westlake and his wife became interested in the Social Credit movement, but were unsuccessful in persuading the Order of Woodcraft Chivalry to align themselves with the Greenshirts, the Order firmly adhering to its democratic, egalitarian principles. See Prynn, p. 235.
21. See Evans, p. 77.
22. *Comradeship and Wheatsheaf*, No. 354 (Dec., 1925), p. xiii.

23.   Leslie Paul (1905-   ). See Biographical Notes.
24.   Clifford Troke, 'Building a New Movement', *The Millgate Monthly* (May, 1935), p. 28.
25.   See Leslie Paul to Joseph Reeves, 21 January 1925 to 5 August 1925, Woodcraft Folk Headquarters, Tooting, London.
26.   See Leslie Paul, 'Early Days of the Woodcraft Folk, A Personal Memoir', 1974 typed Ms., p. 10. Copy kindly sent to me by John Hodgson.
27.   'Woodcrafters in Council', *Comradeship and Wheatsheaf* (Feb., 1926), p. xix.
28.   Anon. (Leslie Paul), 'A History of the Woodcraft Folk', Federation of Co-op Woodcraft Fellowships (n.d.), leaflet, Youth Movement Archive.
29.   E.g., Paul announced that the Wheatsheaf Fellowship movement was 'the only one in which the philosophies of eugenics and Socialism are united and working in harness. We cannot see that it is any use reaching a co-operative commonwealth *if it is inhabited by a degenerating race*' (author's italics). Echoing Baden-Powell, but from an opposing political stand-point, Paul concludes: 'You cannot get A1 Socialism from C3 people.' Paul, 'Greensward: a Woodcraft Log: the seed and the soil', *Comradeship and Wheatsheaf* (April, 1925), p. xix.
30.   Leslie Paul, *The Folk Trail* (London, 1929), pp. 22-23.
31.   See Eileen Totten, 'Scouting with girls, Guiding with boys: on the break-away Woodcraft Folk', the *Guardian*, 7 November 1973; *Annual Report of the National Council of the Woodcraft Folk*, membership returns, 1974, p. 3.
32.   Source: Prynn, p. 289.
33.   From 1933 the Woodcraft Folk received an annual grant of only £10 from the Education Executive of the Co-operative Union, whereas £1,000 was given to a Jubilee Youth Fund in 1935, thus indirectly subsidising the mass British youth movements. In 1936 the Woodcraft Folk unsuccessfully petitioned the Co-operative Union's executive for a grant of £100 towards a national organizer. See *Co-operative News*, 13 December 1936; 11 May 1935; Anon., *Does Co-operation Want Youth?* (London, 1937), pamphlet published by British Federation of Co-operative Youth and Woodcraft Folk.
34.   See Paul Wilkinson, p. 176; information also supplied in conversation by Gerald Davies, 28 December 1975, Publicity Secretary, Woodcraft Folk Headquarters, Tooting, London.
35.   Leslie Paul, *The Republic of Children* (London, 1938), p. 29.

CONCLUSION

One function of youth movements, whatever forms of outdoor activity they may have taken on the surface, was to smooth the way for upper-working-class and lower-middle-class assimilation into the urban-industrial order of British society. Even Baden-Powell reluctantly admitted that Scouting was more popular with boys from this social background in London and the South East than with the working-class in the industrial North and Midlands.[1] For youth movements helped to absorb the upwardly aspiring into the ranks above them in the status hierarchy: by training boys to become accustomed to a new social identity with the minimum of disturbance to the class fabric of society. For the socially ambitious, hard working apprentice, a youth movement became an intermediary, providing a *rite de passage* between and within classes: the equivalent for the adolescent of his younger brother's membership of a Sunday School or Band of Hope.[2]

> Anyone who will take the trouble to enquire personally into the matter, [wrote Lord Roberts to the Earl of Meath in 1898] cannot fail to recognize the benefit conferred on the boys who belong to the [Boys'] Brigade. Not only are they cleaner, brighter, and better mannered than boys of their class generally, *which shows that they have risen above their fellows on the social scale*, but those by whom they are employed bear strong testimony to their increased usefulness and their uniform good conduct.[3] (My italics.)

From the boy's point of view, which is often overlooked, belonging to a youth movement could also encourage self-respect; a process assisted by acquiring badges and wearing a uniform. ' "I'm not a 'know-nothing' that nobody wants to know *now* – I'm a somebody. And if I work hard enough I can be a King's Scout. I'm something now," ' might have been the typical response of a working-class boy in the North London of the 1920s. ' "I can hold my head up as well as him that's gone to the Latymer [Grammar] School." '[4] To the potential employer, on the other hand, the 'steadiness' and sober, Church-going habits which, ideally, the Boys' Brigade 'method' encouraged in its recruits through Bible Class and military drill, were a recommendation of employee reliability. If he were also an Elder in the local Kirk, this

121

assumption was even more likely to be made.⁵ By joining a youth
movement, that is, a boy could almost guarantee himself a 'meal-
ticket' for the future, although such conscious calculation is unlikely
to have influenced many new recruits. Conversely, over-reliance upon
documentary materials and oral evidence garnered from those who
largely held positions of authority has, perhaps, tended to conceal the
more evasive and often potentially subversive methods that boys
could adopt to deflect and undermine well-meaning, if maladroit,
middle-class attempts to maintain order and discipline in a youth
movement. It oversimplifies an undoubtedly much more complex
relationship to assume that the membership received the doctrines of
its adult leadership quite passively without first transmuting their
'message' through an adolescent's set of cultural assumptions derived
from social class and normative reference groups.

Yet a Scout Troop or a Boys' Brigade Company could also serve to
structure an adolescent's individual social status within the wider
national framework of the predominantly middle-class social culture:

> I was chiefly concerned with putting into them [Boy Scouts] what
> we called the Scout spirit, [claimed the 1920s Scout Commissioner
> for Scotland] something of what we call the public school spirit,
> which makes a boy play up and play the game for his side:
> something of what we call *esprit de corps*, which makes men do
> great deeds for their Regiment, forgetting themselves — and very
> much of what we call patriotism.⁶

But in the second quarter of the twentieth century, with the extension
of secondary education and mass communications reinforcing
popular commitment to national norms and values, alternative forms
of affirming social and political respectability became more readily
available. Consequently, youth movements made less of an appeal to
the upwardly mobile than before, while their role as agencies of social
management became increasingly superfluous. Only the lower-middle
classes, with their status anxieties, patriotism and political assertive-
ness, continued during the inter-war period to provide leaders with
enthusiasm at a local level. For them, involvement in a youth movement could act as a form of vicarious identification with middle-class
values, a method of overcoming the uncertainty of their social
standing.⁷ While there is still no general consensus about the sort of
people who became youth leaders in the past, it is reasonable to
conclude, using occupation as an indication of social class, that Scout

leaders today are a predominantly middle-class group.[8]

Did youth movements achieve their manifest aims, or were these aims rapidly subsumed in the means adopted to realize them? Measurement of the success of such voluntary organizations in reaching their self-declared goals is made difficult by the different responses of various social classes, age groups and geographical localities to the directions and commands of their centralized leaderships. Moreover, the aims of national authority, practice at a local level, and the expectations of the boys or their parents, are likely to have had little in common. For while Baden-Powell saw Scouting as developing 'manliness' and 'character' in place of 'loafing' or 'rowdiness', there is little evidence to suggest that the actual form his method of training assumed had any impact on the subsequent ethical or social behaviour of its members.[9] An important motive in the formation of the Boy Scout movement was the defence of the British Empire against threats of both moral and physical decadence. Yet, in practice, the idea of Scouting itself, was both flexible and universal enough in its application for the means of woodcraft and outdoor games to supersede Baden-Powell's wider national purpose of racial regeneration and the elimination of class conflict.

A youth movement also offered a potential mechanism for the maintenance of class stability modelled on the public schools, which had already proved so effective an instrument of social integration for the mid-Victorian business classes and the gentry. Certainly, the leaders of the major British youth movements constantly stressed their ability to provide for working boys that which a public-school education had made available to their more privileged counterparts:

> These lads have had a sound elementary education, but the [Church Lads'] Brigade aims at giving them something hitherto denied them — something of the free discipline, the manly games, the opportunities of wholesome society which a Public School gives.[10]

Until the early 1930s, the Church Lads' Brigade drew its officers almost exclusively from a public-school background.[11] The Boy Scouts inherited much of Baden-Powell's enthusiasm for the public-school Christian manliness he had absorbed as a schoolboy at Charterhouse:

> We, in the Scout Movement, [he pronounced] are credited with supplying for the boy who has not had the same chance as one brought up in a public school an equivalent character training,

especially in the directions of responsibility and discipline.[12]

With equal conviction, William Smith firmly believed that the Boys' Brigade would engender 'that *esprit de corps* which public school boys acquire as a matter of course but which was almost entirely lacking in elementary schoolboys.'[13]

The model adolescent, therefore, became the organized, disciplined, boarding-school youth, dependent but secure from temptation; while the independent and precocious working-class young were stigmatized as delinquent. 'The Boy Scout at 19 will be something very different from the cigarette-smoking street-corner loafer, who diversifies his indolence by occasional bursts of hooliganism. He will be smart, clean, alert, well-mannered.'[14] To further ensure that the rising generation would become loyal, obedient, respectful of law-and-order and disciplined, 'good citizenship' became the ultimate aim of voluntary social education. 'The subject to be instilled must be made to appeal,' confessed Baden-Powell, 'that was my object in suggesting the gilt of "Scouting" for the pill of education in manliness or good citizenship.'[15] The 'good citizen' was one who submitted to authority and learnt rifle-shooting in preparation for war, but shunned cigarette-smoking, self-abuse and drink:

> A Boy Scout can go anywhere, because he is self-reliant, useful and manly, [observed a Scout brochure] he is a good son, because he is taught the necessity of being obedient to those placed in authority over him. He grows up into a sober man because he has learnt the evils of intemperance. You will never see a Boy Scout lounging about the streets, with his hands in his pockets, puffing a cigarette.[16]

Together with other social and cultural influences, Scouting also had some part to play in encouraging a patriotic response to national crisis, of a type indicated by the mass volunteering of the young on the outbreak of the First World War.[17]

How significant were the close historical links which most youth movements maintained with the British military establishment? A deferential regard for the soldier was most commonly expressed through a use of the nomenclature and methods of military training. In 1912 Sir Iain Hamilton called upon youth movements to be 'honest' and recognize that they were not just 'playing a silly game' but had 'a direct bearing on war and on the defence on the country.'[18] It has even been argued that the Boys' Brigade succeeded in instilling military values into the minds of hundreds of thousands of Nonconformists and that by doing so, it also helped pave the way for the recruiting drives of the First World War.[19] While largely owing to the leadership of Baden-Powell, who was, of course, a well-known soldier, the Boy Scouts were constantly being accused of militarism. The Scout movement also came into being at the same time as Parliament was discussing a lecture given by Baden-Powell to his Territorial officers in Newcastle on the need to prepare against the threat of a German invasion.[20] Many of the early Scout Commissioners held military rank or were advocates of the conscriptionist National Service League,[21] as were the Chairmen of certain provincial Scout Associations.[22] To liberal idealists like Sir Francis Vane, this infiltration of pro-conscriptionists into the highest levels of Scouting automatically provided strong grounds for suspecting the purity of their motives.[23] Baden-Powell himself defended the appointment of so many military men to high positions in his movement by arguing that, through early retirement, they were foremost amongst the qualified 'gentlemen' possessing the leisure, training and inclination for such voluntary work.[24]

In the late-nineteenth and early-twentieth centuries, youth work in Britain came to be the voluntary effort of groups of people outside of the social class and age groups of those they organized. Youth movements were, in effect, a mass leisure outlet for the young working-class adolescent controlled by the largely middle-class, middle-aged adult. In acting voluntarily, the pioneers in this field of social training for the young ruled out the alternatives of either unregulated commercial enterprise or working-class self-help.[25] With the end result that youth movements managed the young according to the then culturally dominant middle-class outlook:

> There is no organization which I have found influence so powerfully for good the boys in such a neighbourhood. [Wrote Octavia Hill of a company of her cadets in Notting Hill.] The cadets learn the duty and dignity of obedience; they get a sense of corporate life and of civic duty; they learn to honour the power of endurance and effort . . . and they come in contact with manly and devoted officers . . . These ideals are in marked contrast with the listless self-indulgence, the pert self-assertion, the selfishness and want of reverence, which are so characteristic of the life in a low district.[26]

The patronizing rejection of urban working-class culture and values made explicit here suggests that the middle-class benefactors or activists involved in youth movements set out to mould the leisure of the 'unenlightened' young into the more amenable and familiar shape of their own 'superior' way of life. Inheriting the Octavia Hill approach, in the mid-1930s, a Colonel believed that his experience in the Army had given him an insight into the 'class' of boy with which he had to deal in a cadet company attached to a working boys' club:

> It does not surprise me to hear . . . that they do not show any public spirit and are apt to let you down, it is the nature of this class of boy to do so and one of the aims of Sherborne House is to try and correct this as far as possible.[27]

Youth movements, that is, could act as important institutional vehicles for the transmission of the ideological hegemony.

Until the formation of the left-wing woodcraft groups in the 1920s, youth movements conditioned the young to accept the social order as it was, rather than to make any attempt at changing it. Yet within such constraints, to the individual member they offered potential opportunities for social adjustment, albeit through the internalization of the middle-class values sanctioned by the leadership. A youth movement, at a particular stage in its development, could serve instrumentally as an agency either for hegemony or for social mobility. Equally, a combination of both socially manipulative processes might predominate as the characteristic shaping influence guiding the history of a movement. If, however, such general explanations are insufficient to account for what was happening at a local level, this may be a result of the historian too often gaining his perspective on voluntary organizations from the archival sources of central authority. Thus, if the one publicly expressed goal of British youth movements up until 1940 was that they set out to change the 'moral character' of the individual boy, their unintentional effect may have been felt more in broader terms of social change. Youth movements were a form of recreation enjoyed by the upper-working-class and the lower-middle-class taking place largely under the supervision of the middle-class, who used them as a means for accustoming the membership to accept and to find a place within an evolving urban-industrial society.

Notes

1. See Baden-Powell, 'The Boy Scouts' in *National Defence*, Vol. IV, No. 17 (Aug., 1910), p. 447. Of the 11,000 Scouts in London at this time, Baden-Powell calculated that about half or more came from the lower-middle-class. See J. O. Springhall, 'The Boy Scouts, Class and Militarism in relation to British Youth Movements, 1908-1930' in *International Review of Social History*, Vol. XVI (1971), Pt. 2, Section II; Appendix IV, 'Density of Boy Scouts in Selected Counties for the 1921 Census' indicates that the Home Counties had a higher density of Scouts per thousand teenagers than the industrial North.

2. See Thomas W. Laquer, *Religion and Respectability: Sunday Schools and Working Class Culture, 1780-1850* (London, 1976); A. P. Wadsworth, 'The First Manchester Sunday Schools' in M. W. Flinn and T. C. Smout (eds.), *Essays in Social History* (Oxford, 1974), pp. 100-122; Lilian Shiman, 'The Band of Hope Movement: respectable recreation for working class children', *Victorian Studies*, Vol. XVII, No. 1 (Sept., 1973), pp. 49-74.

3. Lord Roberts to the 12th Earl of Meath, 18 January 1898, Meath Papers, Letters Vol. III, No. 126: Killruddery, Bray, Co. Dublin, Ireland.

4. Cited: G. G. Wilkinson, ex-Scoutmaster, 2nd Edmonton Troop, interviewed 2 January 1973, Edmonton, London.

5. One informant, Norman Vance, tells me in a letter that his grandfather, an Elder in Whiteabbey Church, near Glengormley, Northern Ireland, who owned a wholesale business in Belfast, always claimed – at times erroneously – that the best boys he employed in his warehouse turned out to be BB boys.

6. Major F. M. Crum, *With Riflemen, Scouts and Snipers, 1914-1919* (Oxford, 1921), Appendix I, p. xix. Crum's papers are in the National Library of Scotland.

7. See John Gillis, *Youth and History* (London, 1974), pp. 168-170; idem., 'The Evolution of Juvenile Delinquency in England, 1890-1914', *Past and Present*, No. 67 (May, 1965), pp. 111-113. As one method of affirming social respectability, Gillis points out that teachers were a white-collar group particularly active in the youth work of this period.

8. A recent survey of nearly 500 Scouters by the Management Sciences Department of the University of Manchester Institute of Science and Technology, showed that overall Scouters are better educated than average: 36 per cent having attended a grammar school and 8 per cent having had a private education, 85 per cent receiving further education beyond school. In occupational terms, 53 per cent were in managerial, professional or non-manual jobs, whilst only 8 per cent did semi-skilled or unskilled manual work. Almost half earned more than £3,000 p.a. and 8 per cent more than £4,500. See R. J. Davy, D. W. M. Elliott, D. B. L. Stevens, *To Establish the Leadership Profile and Attitudes of Scout Leaders in order to expand the movement into areas deprived of Scouting*, UMIST, June, 1975, chap. 3.

9. A recent study of Outward Bound and Duke of Edinburgh Award Scheme courses reaches a similar conclusion. See Kenneth Roberts, Graham White, Howard Parker, *The Character Training Industry: adventure training schemes in Britain* (Newton Abbot, 1974), chap. 7. But there was a marked improvement in Sunday School attendance as a result of the activities of the Boys' Brigade. See *Minutes of Conference of Officers of Companies*

in Belfast and District, 22 February 1890, Public Record Office of Northern Ireland, Belfast, T. 1773.

10. Anon., 'General Objects', Church Lads' Brigade, *Fifth Annual Report, 1896-1897*, London, n.p.

11. Taped interview with A. J. Ormiston, ex-CLB Captain, St Margaret's Co., Twickenham, Middlesex, 15 September 1971. Unfortunately, officers' nomination forms for the CLB were destroyed by enemy action during the Second World War.

12. Baden-Powell, 'The Responsibilities of Citizenhood', *The Scouter*, June 1918, cited in W. S. Adams, *Edwardian Portraits* (London, 1957), pp. 132-133.

13. William Smith cited in Bernard Davies and Alan Gibson, *The Social Education of the Adolescent* (London, 1967), p. 43.

14. The *Evening Standard*, 24 January 1911.

15. Baden-Powell, *Scouting for Boys* (London, 1909 edn.), p. 293.

16. Anon., *The Boy Scouts: what they are, what they do, and what Scouting does for them* (n.d., 1909?), p. 4: Vol. I, Ref. 91, Scout Archives, London.

17. On 1 September 1914, Dr T. S. Lukis, Scoutmaster of the Toynbee Hall Troop of Boy Scouts in Whitechapel, placed himself at the head of about 80 of the older Scouts of East London and marched them to the nearest Army recruiting office where he enlisted them *en masse*. See Anon., *A History of the Toynbee Hall Troop of Boy Scouts, 1908-1923* (London, 1923), p. 9.

18. Iain Hamilton, *National Life and National Training* (London, 1913), pp. 19-22. From a speech delivered in Birmingham on 24 September 1912. As Adjutant-General in 1910, Hamilton had helped to draw up the controversial new cadet regulations.

19. See H. J. Hanham, 'Religion and Nationality in the Mid-Victorian Army', in M. R. D. Foot (ed.), *War and Society* (London, 1973), pp. 173-174.

20. See *Hansard*, Parliamentary Debates, 4th Ser., (Commons), Vol. CLXXXVIII, 13 May 1908, questions, cols. 1122-1123; the *Newcastle Daily Chronicle*, 4 May 1908. The talk also ill-advisedly referred to Germany as 'the natural enemy of this country.'

21. 'When the Scout Council was created all the chiefs of the National Service League were brought in.' Vane to Pixley, 17 October 1910: British Boy Scouts File II, Scout Archives, London. See Sir Francis Vane, *The Boy Knight* (London, 1910), p. 15.

22. Viz., Major James, Chairman of the Oxford Boy Scouts Association (1908-1909), and his successor, Sir Montagu Burrows (1909-1935), were both on the executive of the local branch of the National Service League before 1914. See *Minutes, Executive Committee, Oxford Boy Scouts Association*, 1909, Dep. d. 50, Bodleian Library, Oxford.

23. E.g., Vane felt that Sir Edmund Elles, Chief Scout Commissioner (1909-1922), was only interested in the Boy Scouts for the purpose of getting recruits for the Territorials, on whose National Council the latter sat. Elles was also on the executive committee of the National Service League. See Sir Francis Vane, *'Agin the Governments* (London, 1929), p. 210.

24. See Baden-Powell, *Scouting for Boys* (London, 1935 edn.), pp. 318-319. In 1910, out of 250 Presidents and Commissioners of Boy Scouts, 140 were classified as military officers, both serving and retired; by 1912, out of a total of 352, there were 247 military men running the Scouts in Britain. See Lists of Scout Personnel in *The Headquarters Gazette*, Vol. II

(April, 1910), p. 19; and Vol. III (Dec., 1910), pp. 16-19; Anon. (Captain Noemo), *The Boy Scout Bubble* (London, 1912), p. 7.
25. See Davies and Gibson, pp. 31-33.
26. Octavia Hill, *Letter to my Fellow Workers* (London, 1910), pp. 11-12.
27. Colonel Moberley in a *Report of a Meeting at Sherborne of Old Shirburnian Society to consider present state of affairs at Sherborne House,* 3 March 1935. Collection of Colonel Sherbrooke Walker, North Cadbury, Somerset.

APPENDIX 1   GIRLS IN UNIFORM

Basically derivative products of the early-twentieth century, youth movements for girls are, at least in origin, imitations of the organizations originally intended solely for boys. If they are relegated here to the afterthought of an appendix, this is not intended as a comment on their intrinsic interest to the social historian. For example, a detailed investigation of their common Edwardian backgrounds might tell us a great deal about the emergence of the more independent, if still respectable, woman, whose self-assertiveness could find a convenient outlet as an officer in a girls' youth movement.

The first of the uniformed organizations for girls to get off the ground was the Girls' Guildry, forerunner of the present-day Girls' Brigade. Started at the turn of the century, its birthplace, like that of the Boys' Brigade, was in Glasgow. The founder, Dr William Francis Somerville, was the son of a Free Church Minister, whom he had accompanied while a boy on Evangelical missions to Canada and Europe. Both a pioneer radiologist and neurologist, in the mid-1890s he had set up a practice in the West End of Glasgow, while also running a private nursing home. Dr Somerville was a zealous Churchman, the Superintendent of a Sunday School and much concerned about the lack of provision for girls between their leaving Sunday School and becoming communicants. He both knew and admired the Boys' Brigade, which had been started nearby in the 1880s, and shared with others the idea of running a similar scheme for adolescent girls. Then, in early 1900, the smartly dressed Dr Somerville translated thought into action by inviting the older girls in his Sunday School to attend a meeting in the Anderston Church Hall, which was to initiate the Girls' Guildry.[1]

The Girls' Guildry was a unique combination of a senior Sunday School class, friendly club and a female equivalent of the Boys' Brigade. It followed the Boys' Brigade example even to the extent of adopting the marching and military drill so popular at the time of the Boer War. The girls were each dressed in navy blue shirt, straw hat, white blouse and red sash with a symbolic Eastern lamp as their badge. The aim of the Girls' Guildry — to develop in girls, 'capacities of womanly helpfulness' — was given full rein during the First World War in their work for the Red Cross. By 1903 there were already 24 companies in Scotland but only seven in England, where the movement was at first unpopular owing to the straw 'boater' the girls wore being regarded as a badge of the charity school. Although the Girls' Guildry arrived at a time when women were beginning to play a more conspicuous role in society, it was still an affront to those who believed in the fragility of their sex, in that it encouraged unladylike behaviour among tender, 'sensitive' young girls.

In 1939, the Girls' Guildry had a total membership of about 24,000. Of the 475 companies in Britain, 338 were in Scotland, 131 in England and 3 each in Wales and Northern Ireland. In the mid-1960s, the Girls' Guildry, Girls' Life Brigade and Girls' Brigade of Ireland, united to form the Girls' Brigade, now officially the sister movement to the Boys' Brigade. Betraying their Evangelical origins, the new amalgamated movement declared that it was their duty:

> to help girls to resist the temptations surrounding them, in particular to provide positive teaching on the Christian attitude to sex, and to make them aware of the dangers of alcohol, gambling, smoking and undisciplined conduct in their growing and adult lives.[2]

At this time, there were about 100,000 girls under 21 in the Girls' Brigade.

Britain's largest youth association is the Girl Guide movement. There are altogether more than three quarters of a million Brownies, Guides and Rangers. One in four girls aged between seven and ten is now a Brownie, while an estimated 60 per cent of British women have been Girl Guides at one time or another in their lives.[3] In the post-permissive environment of the 1970s, the Girl Guides are flourishing as never before. The Guides owe their origin to a group of 'Girl Scouts' who turned up uninvited — wearing Scout hats, scarves and carrying staves — at the first big rally of Boy Scouts at Crystal Palace in September 1909, demanding to be inspected by Baden-Powell.[4] Initially, the Chief Scout had stood out against girls joining in a game he had principally intended for boys, reasoning that the presence of girls, or even younger children, would act as a deterrent to male adolescent membership. But in the face of feminine persistence he admitted defeat, and, together with his sister Agnes, he wrote *Girl Guides: a suggestion for character training for girls,* which warned of the moral and physical decadence threatening the nation and the difficulties of getting good servants in such a crisis.[5] The Girl Guides were presented as one step among others to counteract such social evils, differing in aim and

detail from the Boy Scouts to suit their sex. Next, Baden-Powell
asked Agnes, a woman thoroughly Victorian in outlook, to take over
the running of the new organization, placing £100 at her disposal as
capital. A small room in Scout Headquarters was rented to serve as an
office, a secretary was engaged and a committee was organized from
among Agnes's elderly spinsterish friends. Their ideas were clearly not
in touch with the rising generation of girls.[6]

When their books were opened in May 1910, and the self-styled
'Girl Scouts' invited to register as Girl Guides, over 8,000 made the
transition — despite the initial unpopularity of the new name which too
patently differentiated them from the Boy Scouts. Then, in 1912,
Agnes, with the collaboration of her famous brother, wrote a handbook
for the Girl Guides adapted from *Scouting for Boys*, with the characteristic title: *How Girls Can Help Build up the Empire.* The result was a
tepid and uninspiring programme and the movement began to flounder.
Because of Agnes's poor organization, the Girl Guides got off to a shaky
start before the First World War, and Baden-Powell himself was too
preoccupied with the Boy Scouts to give much attention to their sisters'
problems. The general situation was not made any easier by a prejudice
which then existed against anything which, even unconsciously, could
be seen as a part of the general movement towards women's rights —
the suffragettes being particularly militant in the late 1900s.[7] But in
1915, Baden-Powell secured a Charter of Incorporation for the Girl
Guides which made them secure from take-over; since Agnes had
almost agreed that they should be swallowed up by the more dynamic
YWCA. Transferring Agnes to the less active and interfering role of
President, Baden-Powell then made himself Chairman of the Guides and
set up a new committee of younger women to run the movement on a
day-to-day basis.[8]

The outbreak of the First World War led to women playing a greater
role in industry and the economy, making it more urgent for the Girl
Guides to organize on a nation-wide scale. Baden-Powell's remodelling
of the movement along decentralized Scout lines proved remarkably
effective and membership soared. In 1916 his young wife, Olave, became
County Commissioner for Sussex and in 1918 she was made Chief Guide.
Baden-Powell, meanwhile, rewrote the Guide Handbook in 1917 as
Girl Guiding (1918), discarding much of the Victorian outlook and pre-
judices of Agnes's earlier contribution. In 1914 the 'Rosebuds' became
known as the Brownies, now Brownie Guides — the most popular of all
the British youth movements for the under-eleven age group.[9] The
first International Guide Conference was held in Oxford in 1920, and at

the sixth, in 1930, Lady Baden-Powell was proclaimed World Chief Guide — an office in which she has served for over 40 years, bringing to the Girl Guides a charismatic personality similar to that which her husband brought to the Boy Scouts.[10]

Notes

1. Cf. Marion Lockhead, *A Lamp was Lit: Girls' Guildry through fifty years* (Edinburgh, 1949), chap 2, *passim.* Other sources give Gilmorehill Church as its birth-place in Glasgow.

2. James H. Leicester and W. A. James Farndale (eds.), *Trends in the Services for Youth* (London, 1967), p. 212.

3. See Celia Haddon, 'The Great Brownie Boom', *Sunday Times,* 9 September 1973; Wendy Hughes, 'It's Boom Year for Brownies', ibid., 12 October 1975; Penny Hunter Symon, 'As Good as a Backwoodsman', *The Times,* 3 March 1971, on Lady Olave Baden-Powell, the World Chief Guide.

4. Alix Liddell, *Sixty Years of Growing: diamond jubilee, 1910-1970* (London, 1970), n.p.

5. See Agnes Baden-Powell and Robert Baden-Powell, *Girl Guides: a suggestion for character training for girls,* (n.d.), p. 4, Scout Archives, Vol. II, ref. 49.

6. See the autobiography of Olave, Lady Baden-Powell as told to Mary Drewery, *Window on my Heart* (London, 1973), p. 108. The Chairman of this committee, the formidable Mrs Lumley-Holland, made even Baden-Powell nervous when he set out to obtain her resignation.

7. See Andrew Rosen, *Rise Up Women! The militant campaign of the Women's Social and Political Union, 1903-1914* (London, 1974).

8. See Mary Drewery, *Baden-Powell: the man who lived twice* (London, 1975), pp. 111-112; William Hillcourt, *Baden-Powell* (London, 1964), p. 352.

9. Although they appeal more to children of parents from the higher social classes. See E. J. Dearnaley and Margaret H. Fletcher, 'Cubs and Brownies: social class, intelligence and interests', *Educational Research,* Vol. X, No. 2, (Feb., 1968), pp. 149-151.

10. Other uniformed youth movements for girls include: the Church Girls' Brigade (1901), a girls' equivalent of the Church Lads' Brigade; the Girls' Life Brigade (1902-1964), a sister movement to the Boys' Life Brigade; the British Camp Fire Girls (1921), an offshoot of the American (1914) organization; the Jewish Girls' Brigade (1963), started belatedly through an initiative from the Jewish Lads' Brigade Liverpool Company; and the Girls' Venture Corps (1964), which incorporates the Girls' Training Corps and the Womens' Junior Air Corps.

APPENDIX II

U.K. Scout Membership by Sections, 1912-41 *

Year	Cubs	Sea Scouts Scouts	Rovers	Warrant-Officers Scoutmasters	Totals
1912		128,397		4,866	138,715
1913		137,776		14,557	152,333
1917	28,450	154,774		13,706	196,930
1918	38,513	145,880		9,995	194,388
1919	46,172	153,376	5,580	13,090	218,218
1920	55,347	155,671	7,263	14,477	232,758
1921	61,315	152,521	7,638	15,601	237,075
1922	69,446	157,966	8,938	17,820	254,170
1923	78,661	161,339	11,603	18,507	270,110
1925	86,720	172,821	17,301	21,977	298,819
1926	87,831	178,848	19,257	23,329	309,265
1927	94,458	186,572	20,790	24,248	326,068
1928	115,083	190,186	23,944	27,761	356,974
1929	134,179	193,492	25,565	30,261	383,497
1930	155,576	201,228	31,111	34,747	422,662
1931	160,991	206,818	34,561	37,673	440,043
1932	161,533	218,550	38,735	40,463	459,281
1933	158,741	222,229	38,927	41,843	461,740
1934	151,141	211,195	35,809	42,064	440,209
1935	149,087	204,058	33,464	41,302	427,911
1936	146,523	200,660	35,268	40,543	422,994
1937	147,882	201,103	31,194	41,625	421,804
1938	156,657	206,682	31,276	44,098	438,713
1941	110,959	158,268	9,715	21,082	300,024

* Source: *Scout Annual Census* (adapted)

APPENDIX III

U.K. Boys' Brigade Membership by Sections, 1912-41*

Year	Boy Reservest Life Boys (under 12)	Boys' Brigade	Officers	Totals	Companies
1912		55,819	6,039	61,858	1,298
1913		59,714	6,138	65,852	1,282
1914		60,244	6,503	66,747	1,360
1915		63,375	6,754	70,127	1,369
1916		55,601	6,368	61,969	1,346
1917		48,124	5,685	53,809	1,184
1918	1,573	46,586	4,947	53,106	1,078
1919	3,385	43,563	4,753	51,701	991
1920	5,998	51,584	5,653	63,235	1,181
1921	6,856	52,748	5,851	65,455	1,199
1922	8,406	56,784	6,264	71,454	1,239
1923	9,957	57,240	6,451	73,648	1,267
1924	12,632	58,360	6,708	77,700	1,329
1925	16,911	60,280	7,215	84,406	1,380
1926	18,928	60,222	7,437	86,587	1,436
1927**	25,714	78,450	9,499	113,663	2,075
1928	29,129	79,772	10,117	119,018	2,157
1929	33,625	79,948	10,218	123,791	2,209
1930	42,085	79,339	10,467	131,891	2,257
1931	48,331	79,364	11,079	138,774	2,326
1932	51,701	85,033	11,500	148,234	2,395
1933	52,219	92,804	12,269	157,292	2,510
1934	53,607	96,762	12,808	163,177	2,628
1935	50,848	92,509	12,481	155,838	2,673
1936	50,310	91,479	12,810	154,599	2,717
1937	51,027	91,067	12,685	154,779	2,734
1938	53,150	92,138	12,718	158,006	2,750
1939	55,365	93,655	12,956	161,976	,821
1940	35,782	76,749	11,718	124,249	2,498
1941	28,910	63,789	10,445	103,144	2,150

*   Source: Figures supplied by Boys' Brigade Records Section.

†   Boy Reserves: 1917-1926; Life Boys: 1926-1967; Junior Section: 1967-

**   Access of numbers owing to 1926 amalgamation with Boys' Life Brigade.

APPENDIX IV

Density of Boy Scouts in Selected Counties for the 1921 Census*

County or city	Population of boys, 10-19 per county	Total no. of Scouts per county	No. of Scouts per thousand of total pop. per county	No. of Scouts per thousand of boys 10-19
London	393,589	33,207	11	84
Cambs.	11,881	982	5	83
Surrey	83,178	6,564	10	79
Herts.	31,969	2,391	10	75
Kent	106,438	7,512	9	71
Isle of Wight	6,906	482	6.5	70
Westmoreland	5,627	386	7	69
Soke of Peterborough	4,100	266	8.5	65
Berks.	28,562	1,800	9	63
Sussex	62,479	3,794	7	61
Birmingham	85,222	4,969	7	58
Oxford	17,457	1,022	7	58.5
Hamps.	83,580	4,807	7	57.5
Hunts.	5,247	289	6	55
Dorset	20,878	1,086	6	52
Wilts.	26,631	1,234	5.5	46
Norfolk	46,364	2,084	4.5	45
Bucks.	23,688	1,054	6	45
Bristol	34,701	1,520	6	44
Devon	61,498	2,754	5.5	45
Somerset	42,065	1,813	6	43
North Riding, Yorks.	44,289	1,868	4.5	42
Suffolk	39,078	1,578	5.5	40

* Source: *Census of England and Wales*, 1921; *Boy Scout Annual Census*, 1922. Before 1921, there was no breakdown of Boy Scout statistics into counties.

APPENDIX V

U.K. Comparative Strengths of Various Youth Movements, 1900-1941

Year	Boy Scouts		Boys' Brigade		Church Lads' Brigade		Army Cadet Force	
	Groups	Totals*	Cos.	Totals[†]	Units	Totals (approx.)	Cos.	Totals (approx.)
1900			906	44,415	1,238			
1901			1,014	51,821	1,326			
1902			1,100	53,725	1,139			
1903			1,148	55,188	1,146			
1904			1,161	55,285	1,186			
1905			1,197	56,893	—			
1906			1,237	58,888	1,259	45,000		11,000
1907			1,267	60,648	—	—		—
1908			1,324	64,134	—	70,000		—
1909			1,396	69,472	—	—		—
1910	3,898	107,986	1,386	68,089	1,379	—		
1911	—	123,904	1,326	63,126	1,363	36,000	251	14,399
1912	4,945	138,715	1,298	61,858	1,321		699	34,474
1913	5,345	152,333	1,282	65,852	1,430		846	41,108
1914	—	—	1,360	66,747	1,557		—	—
1915	—	—	1,369	70,127	1,730		1,411	64,314
1916	—	—	1,346	61,969	1,816		1,620	78,651
1917	6,717	196,930	1,184	53,809	1,869		—	—
1918	6,710	197,030	1,078	53,106	1,936		2,005	105,121
1919	7,434	218,318	991	51,701	2,167		—	—
1920	8,069	232,758	1,181	63,235	2,119		2,423	118,893
1921	—	237,075	1,199	65,455	1,999		2,318	119,706
1922	—	254,170	1,239	71,454	1,955		—	—
1923	—	270,110	1,267	73,648	1,848		—	—
1924	—	282,635	1,329	77,700	1,936		—	—
1925	—	298,819	1,380	84,406	1,994	18,189	953	49,841
1926	—	309,265	1,436	86,587	2,016	—	—	—
1927	—	326,068	2,075	113,663	2,070	—	—	50,000
1928	—	356,974	2,157	119,018	2,123	—	949	49,510
1929	—	383,497	2,209	123,791	—	—	—	—

(cont . . .)

(cont . . .)

Year	Boy Scouts		Boys' Brigade		Church Lads' Brigade		Army Cadet Force	
	Groups	Totals*	Cos.	Totals[†]	Units	Totals (approx.)	Cos.	Totals (approx.)
1930	10,296	422,662	2,257	131,891	1,320	–	–	30,000
1931	10,741	440,043	2,326	138,774	–	20,000	–	23,953
1932	11,259	459,281	2,395	148,234	966	–	–	–
1933	11,505	461,740	2,510	157,292	1,021	–	–	–
1934	11,470	440,209	2,628	163,177	1,022	–	–	
1935	11,372	427,911	2,673	155,838	1,040	–		
1936	11,072	422,994	2,717	154,599	1,051	–		
1937	10,771	421,804	2,734	154,779	1,083			
1938	10,719	438,713	2,756	158,006	1,097			
1939	–	–	2,821	161,976	1,073		–	20,000
1940	–	–	2,498	124,249	945		–	
1941	8,521	300,024	2,150	103,144	951			

* Includes: Cubs, Sea Scouts, Scouts, Rovers, Scoutmasters, Warrant Officers.
† Includes: Boy Reserves/Life Boys, Officers and Boys' Brigade.

CRITICAL BIBLIOGRAPHY

What follows is a selective listing of some printed source materials
relating to particular youth movements. It is not intended to be a
comprehensive bibliography but a list of the principal works which
I have found to yield some information. Further research into youth
movement history has to be conducted largely through the careful
sifting of primary source materials, therefore I have provided as full
a *catalogue raisonné* of the manuscript collections consulted during the
course of my own investigations as possible.

Boys' Brigade

Reliable, if less than penetrating, authorized biographies of the founder
of the Boys' Brigade have been published by the editor of *The Boys'
Brigade Gazette*, F. P. Gibbon, *William A. Smith of the Boys' Brigade*
(London, 1934), and the BB's London Secretary, Roger S. Peacock,
Pioneer of Boyhood: story of Sir William A. Smith (Glasgow, 1954);
both knew Smith well but the former is the more rewarding. For a
general account of the development of the Boys' Brigade there is the
compendious, if superficial, survey by Austin E. Birch, *The Story of
the Boys' Brigade* (London, 1959). I have found an undergraduate
dissertation, Christopher Farmer, 'The Foundation of the Boys'
Brigade: Social Discipline or Heavenly Design?' (Keele, 1973), useful
on the Evangelical background. Recently, Brian M. Fraser of the
University of Strathclyde has embarked on post-graduate research
into the beginnings of the Boys' Brigade.

Other Brigades

The most valuable source on the early history of the Church Lads'
Brigade is the CLB's *Twentieth Anniversary Souvenir of the Church
Lads' Brigade, 1891-1911* (London, 1911), a copy of which is held in
the Youth Movement Archive at Cardiff. A more polemical source is
the Revd Edgar Rogers, *The Making of a Man in the CLB* (London,
1919), while the Revd H. Russell Wakefield's *What is the Church Lads'
Brigade?* (London, 1894) is self-explanatory. There are only passing
references to the other brigades dealt with herein, but the constant
flow of Theodor Herzl biographies usually touch on Colonel Goldsmid
and the Maccabeans, viz. Desmond Stewart (1975), while Sidney

Bunt's *Jewish Youth Work in Britain* (London, 1975), is a well-informed, albeit controversial, guide. The best account of the setting up of the Boys' Life Brigade is given in John Lewis Paton, *John Brown Paton: a biography by his son* (London, 1914).

Boy Scouts

The extensive literature on Scouting needs to be treated with caution as it has been flawed until recently by either an excessive concern for the movement's public image or by an over-adulation of its founder, Baden-Powell. The Boy Scout seal of approval is evident, for example, in such otherwise worthy co-operative efforts as: Henry Collis, Fred Hurll and Rex Hazlewood, *B-P's Scouts: an official history of the Boy Scouts Association* (London, 1961), or the Baden-Powell Memorial Fund's *Baden-Powell Story* (London, 1961). Surprisingly re-issued in 1975 as *The Chief*, Eileen K. Wade's *The Piper of Pax: the life story of Lord Baden-Powell of Gilwell* (London, 1924), is in the mythopoetic class, although her *Twenty-one Years of Scouting* (London, 1929), has some contribution to make on the early years. More competent as an official biography is E. E. Reynolds, *Baden-Powell* (London, 1942), while his *The Scout Movement* (London, 1949), is also an informative source. Numerous earlier biographies of the Chief Scout in a herioc mould were superseded in 1964 with the publication of William Hillcourt with Olave, Lady Baden-Powell, *Baden-Powell: the two lives of a hero* (London, 1964), an all-embracing, lengthy work of careful, if uncritical, scholarship which deserves to be reprinted. An antidote to the generally admiring portrayals of Baden-Powell is the acidulous section on him in W. S. Adams, *Edwardian Portraits* (London, 1957). Recommended as a fascinating straight-forward examination of Scouting from within the movement is P. B. Nevill, *My Scouting Story* (London, 1960). Other memoirs include: F. Haydn Dimmock, *Bare Knee Days* (London, 1937), and the more flamboyant autobiography, *Ralph Reader Remembers* (Folkstone, 1975). A characteristic example of Baden-Powell's own prolific writings can be found in the much-maligned *Rovering to Success* (London, 1922), but the essential starting-off point is his *Scouting For Boys* (London, 1908). The general flavour of Baden-Powell's pronouncements can be tasted in: *B-P's Outlook* (London, 1941), a selection of his articles for *The Scouter*. Not to be overlooked are the countless Scout troop histories which can be consulted in local libraries.

Army Cadet Force

The major source I have mined is a detailed but rather meandering
series of anonymous articles on 'The Cadet Story, 1860-1960',
appearing in *The Cadet Journal and Gazette* from 1959 to 1960. Short
histories of the cadet movement are also given *en passant* in Anon.
(W. L. Newcombe), *The Army Cadet Force Handbook* (London, 1949),
and Lt.-Col. H. C. Hughes, *The Army Cadets of Surrey, 1860-1960*
(London, 1960). A good short history of the important 1st London
Cadet Battalion is that edited by W. F. Airs and J. S. Streeter, *Sixty
Years a Cadet* (London, 1949). Material on the Southwark Cadets can
also be gleaned from C. Edmund Maurice (ed.), *Life of Octavia Hill
as told in her letters* (London, 1913).

Woodcraft Groups

Well-researched and admirably presented accounts of these groups can
be found in two outstanding unpublished M.A. theses: Paul Wilkinson,
'A Study of English Uniformed Youth Movements, 1883-1935: their
origin, development, and social and political influence', 1968,
University of Wales; and David Prynn, 'The Socialist Sunday Schools,
the Woodcraft Folk and Allied Movements', 1971, University of
Sheffield, Vol. II. Earlier works, although lacking the benefit of hindsight, contain much valuable information on the woodcraft groups,
viz., I. O. Evans, *Woodcraft and World Service* (London, 1930), and
Leslie Paul, *The Republic of Children* (London, 1938). The latter's
autobiography, *Angry Young Man* (London, 1951), is also revealing
on the origins of the Woodcraft Folk. The best introduction to the
Kibbo Kift Kindred are the works of its leader, John Hargrave, such as:
The Great War Brings it Home (London, 1919); *The Confession of
Kibbo Kift* (London, 1927) and *Social Credit Clearly Explained*
(London, 1945). Similarly, for the Woodcraft Folk, Leslie Paul
published: *The Folk Trail* (London, 1929); *The Child and the Race*
(London, 1926); and *The Training of Pioneers* (London, 1936).

Girls' Youth Movements

There exists ample room for a full-scale survey of youth movements
directed at recruiting young girls. For the Girls' Guildry, now the
Girls' Brigade, there is only Marion Lockhead, *A Lamp was Lit*
(Edinburgh, 1949), which I found quite helpful on this sister movement
to the Boys' Brigade. A portrait of the founder of the Girls' Guildry,
Dr William Francis Somerville, can be found in Henry Brougham
Morton (ed.), *A Hillhead Album* (Glasgow, 1973). The Girl Guides, as

Britain's largest youth movement, certainly deserves more recognition
from the historian. Little exists, apart from such publicity brochures
as Alix Liddell's souvenir of their 1970 Diamond Jubilee, *Sixty Years
of Growing* (London, 1970), which retails some facts. There is a
rather anodyne biography of Olave, Lady Baden-Powell by Eileen K.
Wade, *World Chief Guide* (London, 1971), preferably to be read in
conjunction with her autobiography as told to Mary Drewery, *Window
on My Heart* (London, 1973), which is often unintentionally revealing.
A potential historian of the Girl Guides could profitably consult such
early manifestos of the movement as: Agnes Baden-Powell and Robert
Baden-Powell, *How Girls Can Help Build Up the Empire* (London,
1912); Roland E. Philipps, *The Patrol System for Girl Guides* (London,
1916); and the basic handbook written by Baden-Powell himself,
Girl Guiding (London, 1918). See also, Rose Kerr, *The Story of the
Girl Guides* (n.d.).

In General

The following studies of voluntary organizations involved with the
training of youth, but not classified here as youth movements, are
worthy of mention: William Mc. G. Eager, *Making Men: a history of
boys' clubs and related movements in Great Britain* (London, 1951);
Arthur Gillette, *One Million Volunteers: the story of Volunteer Youth
Service* (London, 1968); Oliver Coburn, *Youth Hostel Story* (London,
1950); Alicia Percival, *Youth Will Be Led: the story of the voluntary
youth organizations* (London, 1951); Bernard Davies and Alan Gibson,
The Social Education of the Adolescent (London, 1967), particularly
for chap. 2 which offers 'a historical perspective' crammed with
suggestive ideas; Fred Milson, *Youth Work in the 1970's* (London,
1970); Westhill Training College, *Eighty Thousand Adolescents*
(London, 1950), an interesting Free Church College survey of the
youth of Birmingham which often finds it difficult to conceal dis-
approval of their activities; Kenneth Roberts, Graham White, Howard
Parker, *The Character Training Industry: adventure training schemes
in Britain* (Newton Abbot, 1974), in which the Duke of Edinburgh
Award Scheme is ruthlessly examined; James H. Leicester and James
Farndale (eds.), *Trends in the Services for Youth* (London, 1967), an
invaluable and monumental work of reference. On youth in general,
John Gillis, *Youth and History: tradition and change in European age
relations, 1770-present* (London, 1974), is an ambitious attempt to
synthesise changing conceptions of youth; Freidrich Heer, *Challenge of
Youth* (London, 1974), a less successful attempt; F. Musgrove, *Youth*

and the Social Order (London, 1964), an instructive source for demographic and economic influences on the status of the young; Walter Laqueur, *Young Germany* (London, 1962), a pioneering historical survey of the German youth movement; two issues of the *Journal of Contemporary History*, Vol. IV, No. 2 (1969), and Vol. V, No. 1 (1970), contain a series of relevant articles on 'Generations in Conflict', Zig Layton-Henry has recently published articles in this journal on party political youth movements in Britain.

Manuscript Collections

Army Cadet Force Association, London

A few miscellaneous records and press cuttings; but otherwise disappointing, since the Association was only formed in 1930.

Baden-Powell House, London

The Library holds a full collection of Baden-Powell's published works and other Scout literature. An archive in the basement contains abundant material on Mafeking and Jamboree Camps, as well as family scrapbooks, photograph albums and some original manuscripts.

Bodleian Library, Oxford

Minute Books and records of the Oxford Boy Scouts Association, 1909-1926, Dep. d. 50-60; and Oxford University Boy Scout Club, 1919-1943, Ms. Top. Oxon. 328/1-3. Useful for tracing National Service League connections with Scouting at a provincial level. Some Baden-Powell correspondence.

Boys' Brigade Headquarters, Fulham, London

Invaluable collection of Smith family papers and correspondence, including William Smith's letter books, 1885-1887, and record of the negotiations with the War Office, 1910-1911. Archive also contains particulars of officers and enrolment of companies since the 1890s.

Bray, Co. Wicklow, Ireland

Papers and press cuttings collection of the 12th Earl of Meath, founder of the Empire Day Movement, and Scout Commissioner for Ireland from 1911 to 1928. Some correspondence with Baden Powell and other youth leaders in autograph albums.

British Library of Political and Economic Science

Barnett Papers. Octavia Hill to Barnetts, 1873 1906. Of marginal interest for the Southwark Cadets, but revealing about Miss Hill's character and her relationship with Canon Barnett.

British Museum

Baden-Powell Papers, Add. Mss. 50255. Scrappy, largely dealing with Mafeking, but includes diary of 1910-1911 visit to Ireland and some letters.
Cockerell Papers, Add. Mss. 52722. Letters from Octavia Hill, of particular interest in 1900 for Southwark Cadet finances.
Arnold-Foster Papers, Add. Mss. 50275-50357. Of interest for reaction of 'brigades' to General Mackinnon's Committee of 1904, recommending special treatment to army recruits from youth movements.

Cadet Training Centre, Camberley, Surrey

Early enrolment book of Southwark Cadets, 1889-1891, a useful source for the occupational breakdown of boys. Some letters from ex-cadets.

Centre for Military Archives, King's College, London

Hamilton Papers. Correspondence with Baden-Powell, Lord Roberts and Haldane, but chiefly of interest for compulsory military service debate.

Church Commissioners, Millbank, London

Several files of great interest for any investigation of Octavia Hill's management of the Commissioners' Southwark house property, viz. 65065. Also reports and minutes of Estates Committee are useful for Southwark.

Church Lads' Brigade Headquarters, Finchley, London

Minute Books, Executive Committee from 1891. A useful collection of early leaflets, annual reports and assorted material. Disappointing lack of quantifiable information.

Dublin, Ireland (Farney Park)

George Childs Collection. Private collection of papers relating to Boy Scouts, particularly in Ireland, including useful notes on the early history of the Dublin Boy Scouts Association, 1908-1916. Also holds some of Baden-Powell's less accessible early publications.

Enfield, Middlesex

Enfield Central Library. Provides materials from which a history of
Enfield in the late-nineteenth and early-twentieth centuries can be
built up.
Edmonton Central Library. School log books, local history information.
1st Enfield Boys' Brigade Co. Full and invaluable source material for
this company, now in the possession of the present Captain, L. R.
Moody.
Avenue Hall Congregational Church, Minute Books, 1892-1904, Log
Books. Bush Hill Park Church which ran a Boys' Brigade Company.
Ridge Family Papers. Of particular interest for the history of the 1st
Enfield Boys' Brigade Co., local Congregationalism and Dr J. J. Ridge.
In possession of Dr Ben Ridge.

Glasgow Batalion Headquarters, Boys' Brigade

Holds early officers' enrolment forms but otherwise disappointing.
The 1st Glasgow Co. of Boys' Brigade has a collection of records which
were kept, at time of consultation, in the original North Woodside
Mission Hall. Full information on the original company set up by
William Smith in 1883.

Greater London Record Office

Barnett Papers. F/BAR/1-459. Canon Barnett offers a frank opinion of
Octavia Hill in letters to his brother, Francis, 1897-1902. Also holds
surviving Toynbee Hall Records, A/Toy.

Guildhall Library, London

Minute Book, 1908-1913, papers of the City of London Territorial
and Auxiliary Forces Association, General Purposes Committee.
Minute Books, City of London Territorials, Cadet Committee, 1912-
1928, Ms. 12/612. Little of real interest.

Hoare's Bank Archives, Fleet St., London

Annual Reports, 1888 onwards of the 1st London Cadet Battalion.
Also holds Battalion Minute Books, 1922-1933; Notes of Meetings and
Agenda, 1925-1963. A valuable collection of London cadet history,
including some early leaflets and other scattered material.

Hove Public Library, Sussex

Wolseley Papers. Letters between Octavia Hill and Lady Wolseley are a useful source for the setting up of the Southwark Cadet Corps, 1888-1889. Also holds Octavia Hill to Sir Frederick Maurice.

Institute of Civil Engineers, London

Record and Diary Book of the 1st London Cadet Battalion, 1888-1950. Essential for correct chronological development of Battalion's companies. Possession of Lieut.-Colonel P. F. Hurst.

Ipswich and East Suffolk Record Office

Minutes of Executive Committee, 1924-1957, Annual Reports and Accounts, 1923-1960, handbooks, pamphlets and some correspondence of local Scout Association, Acc. No. 29391/GC2. Significant for personality clashes at Commissioner level in 1930s but otherwise offers little.

Islington Central Library, London

Pamphlets and newspaper cuttings related to Scouting in this borough. Of particular rather than general interest. YpB954.

Kent County Archives, Maidstone

Smith-Masters Papers. Scoutmaster in Meopham, Kent, 1910-1911. U1127.
H. J. Benians Papers. Local architect-Scoutmaster, 1920-1922. U1094. Correspondence and Minute Books. Of interest largely for details of the problems and expenses of running a local Scout troop.

Lancing, Sussex

Scout Association Records Office. Records consulted at Buckingham Palace Road offices were transferred here in 1975, including essential scrapbook volumes, 1908-1960. Some Baden-Powell correspondence should have survived the move.

Marylebone Public Library, London

Cockerell Papers. Includes some letters from Octavia Hill with regard to the management of the Southwark Cadets, mostly 1900.

Mitchell Library, Glasgow

Glasgow Room. Useful source for local history of city but disappointing on the Boys' Brigade — surely one of its brightest ornaments — and William Smith, a local celebrity.

Moccatta Library, University College, London

Full collection of Minute Books, 1897-1936, pamphlets and leaflets, deposited by the Jewish Lads' Brigade. As a library of Jewish history and culture it also provides the materials with which to construct the historical background to the Brigade.

National Library of Scotland, Edinburgh

Major F. M. Crum Papers. Acc. 4981. Voluminous collection in several boxes, includes publications, diaries and correspondence. Of particular interest for his 1911 reflections on the early days of Scouting.

North Cadbury, Somerset

Sherbrooke-Walker Papers. Useful for post-1920 development of Southwark Cadet Corps and Sherborne House Boys Club. Includes important report of 1935 meeting to consider future of cadet training in Southwark.

Oxford City Library

Oxfordshire Boy Scouts Association Annual Reports from 1925. Registers of City of Oxford High School can be used to trace local Scoutmasters.

Public Record Office, London

W.O. 32/9. Correspondence between Army Council and Treasury on cost of new cadet force in 1910, Cadets 227/General Policy. Instructive letters on this issue between Adjutant-General Hamilton and Minister for War, Haldane, also on file.

Reigate Heath, Surrey

Nevill Papers. Basic source for pre-1914 history of 5th Enfield (Bush Hill Park) Boy Scout Troop of which Nevill was Scoutmaster and, by extension, for the early history of Scouting in London. Scrapbooks, log books, letters, photograph albums and miscellaneous collection.

Richmond Central Library, Surrey

Local history collection. Contains several celebratory histories of both Scout troops and Boys' Brigade companies written for particular anniversaries. A wealth of similar material exists in local library collections all over Britain.

Ripley, Surrey

Baden-Powell Papers. Collection of present Lord Baden-Powell, includes grand-father's published works and volumes of press-cuttings and miscellaneous materials. The Baden-Powell family papers are in the possession of Francis Baden-Powell, Chelsea, London, awaiting a chronicler.

Roland House Settlement, Stepney Green, London

Log Books of House, 1919-1930, Roland Philipps' letters to Nevill, 1916, and large library of Scout publications. Since the First World War, Roland House has provided a meeting place and lodgings for Scoutmasters in East London.

Royal Arsenal Co-operative Society, London

Minute Books, Education Department. Disappointing source for the Woodcraft Folk, but contains runs of Co operative papers.

Scottish Record Office, Edinburgh

College Free Church, Glasgow, Annual Reports, 1877-1888. A useful source for the activities of the North Woodside mission, home of the first Boys' Brigade Company. The inventory of the personal estate of William Smith held here shows that he had shares in the African Lakes Corporation.

Southwark Central Library, London

Red Cross Hall and Gardens. Annual Reports and collections of related material. Little of interest on cadets but source for local history.

Stoke Newington, London

Bennett Papers. The remaining company of the original 1st London Cadet Battalion holds much interesting material on their early history in Southwark, including Bennett's correspondence and old concert programmes. Consulted by permission of Captain Bill Cross.

Tower Hamlets Central Library, London

Local history collection holds a great deal of material on local boys' clubs in the East End, of particular interest for Jewish working boys' clubs between the wars. Some Scout publications.

Winterborne Zelston, Blandford Forum, Dorset

Bennett Diaries, 1889-1938. Useful indication of day-to-day routine of running a cadet corps. Typical entry: 'dined at Cock, went to S'wark

Club, very rowdy, boys smashed plaster cast of the Queen, slept at Bank' (29 October 1889). In possession of his son, R. L. S. Bennett.

Woodcraft Folk Headquarters, Tooting, London

Archival collection. Includes press cuttings from 1920s, yearbooks, correspondence and miscellaneous publications of Leslie Paul. Gives some insight into the early struggles of the Folk for recognition.

Youth Movement Archive, University College, Cardiff

Started in 1973 on the initiative of Paul Wilkinson, Senior Lecturer in the Politics Department, to offer a repository for the smaller wood-craft movements. The Archive eventually hopes to provide a full range of research materials on youth movement history. Excellent facilities for storage provided by University College Library.

BIOGRAPHICAL NOTES

BADEN-POWELL, Robert Stephenson Smyth, (1857-1941)

Born in London, Baden-Powell's father, who died when Baden-Powell was three, was a Professor of Geometry at Oxford; his mother was one of the daughters of Admiral William Smyth (1788-1865). She was a pioneer in the education of middle-class women, and founder of the Girls' Public Day School Trust. Educated at Rose Hill School, Tunbridge Wells and Charterhouse School (1870-1876), Baden-Powell was with the 13th Hussars in India from 1876 to 1883. On leaving India as a Captain he carried out secret reconnaisance in Basutoland and took part in the 1888 Zulu War against Dinizulu. In 1889 his uncle, General Sir Henry Smyth, the Governor of Malta, made Baden-Powell his Military Secretary and A.D.C., and then Intelligence Officer for the Mediterranean. During the 1895 Ashanti War in West Africa, he commanded a native levy to Kumasi and in 1896 was appointed Chief Staff Officer to Sir Frederick Carrington who crushed the Matabele uprising in Central Africa. In 1897 he was promoted to Colonel-in-command of the 5th Dragoon Guards, a cavalry regiment stationed in India. Lord Wolseley sent him to Africa in 1899 to raise two battalions of Mounted Rifles and to organize the Police Forces on the North West Frontier of Cape Colony. The siege of Mafeking followed . . .

BENNETT, Lancelot, (1865-1949)

Lancelot Bennett was a young city bank clerk who first met Ingham Brooke (q.v.) in 1888 at the Red Cross Boys' Club through a cousin; from 1889 to 1919 he was officer in command of 'B' Company of the Southwark Cadets. Because of his deafness, he was unable to join the Army as he would, apparently, have preferred. In succession Bennett was: Secretary of the Cadets' Club in Union Street, Southwark (1893-1921); Commanding Officer, 1st London Cadet Battalion (1919-1926); Warden of the Southwark Cadet Corps and Sherborne House Boys' Club (1921-1947); Honorary Colonel of the Battalion (1938-1949) and President of the Corps and Club (1949). See L. W. Bennett Diaries, 1889-1938: consulted by kind permission of his son, R. L. S. Bennett, at Winterborne Zelston, Blandford Forum, Dorset.

BROOKE, William Ingham, (18   -1923)

Living among the poor from 1883, Ingham Brooke came to the East
End of London via his father's Yorkshire parsonage and Balliol
College, Oxford. He was in residence at Toynbee Hall from July 1886
until November 1887. A friend of Octavia Hill's (q.v.) through his work
for the COS, on getting married in 1894 he retired from the Southwark
Cadet Corps Company of which he was Captain, was later ordained, and
became Rector of Barford, near Warwick, until his death in 1923. In
1900 as a Vicar in Halifax, Brooke contrasted his career as 'the C.O.S.
secretary, miscellaneous philanthropist and agitator' with that of 'the
mild and gentle High Church parson worried by the vagaries of his
curate.' See Brooke to 'Bruce', 11 December 1900, Toynbee Hall
Records, Greater London Record Office.

COCKERELL, Sydney, (1867-1962)

Sydney Cockerell began his career as a coal merchant. Working for many
years with Octavia Hill, who was rather over-bearing and meticulous in
her supervision of the Southwark Cadets' accounts, in the 1890s Cockerell became Secretary to William Morris and the Kelmscott Press.
Eventually, he graduated to the post of Director of the Fitzwilliam
Museum in Cambridge (1907-1937). See Octavia Hill to Cockerell,
1900-1901: British Museum, Add. Mss. 52722 and Local History Room,
Marylebone Public Library, London.

GOLDSMID, Albert Edward, (1846-1904)

Goldsmid was born in Poona, Bombay, in 1846 to a well-known Indian
Civil Servant. He went to Sandhurst and by 1866 had received a commission in the 104th Bengal Fusiliers. From 1879 he served as a staff
officer in Belfast and London until being granted leave from 1892 to
1894 to help supervise Baron de Hirsch's Jewish settlements in the
Argentine. He was put in command of the 41st or 'Welsh' Regimental
District at Cardiff until 1897 but, when the South African War broke
out, he was made Chief Staff Officer at Aldershot and sent out to
fight on the veldt. On his return he retired at half-pay to devote himself
to the JLB, remaining its Commandant until his death in 1904. See
Obituary in the *Jewish Chronicle*, 1 April 1904, pp. 9-10; Chaim
Bermant, *The Cousinhood* (London, 1971), pp. 242-243.

HAIG-BROWN, The Revd Canon Dr William, (1823-1907)

Haig-Brown was appointed Headmaster of Charterhouse in 1863. A

Fellow of Pembroke College, Cambridge, he went on to take Holy
Orders. His controversial campaign to remove the school from a site
near the new Smithfield Market in London to Godalming in Surrey, met
with considerable resistance from the Governors. It eventually required
an Act of Parliament and was not completed until 1872, Baden-Powell's
second year at the school. Under Haig-Brown, a popular Head who
became known as 'our second founder', the school expanded by 1876
to five hundred. He retired in 1897 to be appointed Master of Charterhouse Hospital in London.

HARGRAVE, John, (1895-   )

John Hargrave was the son of Gordon Hargrave, a nominal Quaker
and landscape painter. By the age of 15 he was working as an illustrator for Nelson's, going on to become cartoonist for the *Evening
Times* at the age of 17; later he worked in advertising. He joined the
staff of Arthur Pearson's (Baden-Powell's publishers) in 1914, having
already published a Scouting manual, *Lonecraft* (1913), dedicated to
Ernest Thompson Seton. He served as a stretcher-bearer in Suvla Bay,
Gallipoli and Salonika, an experience described in his *At Suvla Bay*
(1916), until being invalided out in 1916; when he returned to find
that Scouting was being used as an instrument for waging war on the
domestic front. As Headquarters' Commissioner for Camping and Woodcraft (1916-1920), he appeared to many to be marked out as Baden-
Powell's eventual successor. In his period as a Social Credit propagandist, Hargrave wrote the Alberta Report of 1937 and served as Honorary Advisor to the Alberta Government Planning Commission.
Social Credit Clearly Explained (1945) was his last publication for
Major Douglas. Hargrave's best-remembered achievement was the
founding, in 1920, of the remarkable Kibbo Kift Kindred. See J. L.
Findlay, 'John Hargrave, the Green Shirts and Social Credit', *The
Journal of Contemporary History*, Vol. V, No. 1 (1970), pp. 53-71.

HILL, Octavia, (1838-1912)

A grand-daughter on her mother's side of Dr Thomas Southwood
Smith, the Public Health Commissioner, her father was a failed merchant
banker and her mother ran a private school for girls. About 1852, she
took charge of a group of ragged school children toy-making for the
Ladies' Guild, a Christian Socialist co-operative managed by her mother.
In her twenties, while helping her mother and sisters run their private
school, she also served as the secretary and part-time teacher of classes
for women at Frederick Denison Maurice's Working Men's College in

Great Ormond Street. In 1865, when she was 27, she accepted an offer from John Ruskin to help finance her in a housing experiment by purchasing the leaseholds of three small houses in Marylebone, where she was to act as her own rent-collector. In time, more houses were added and she won acclaim in philanthropic circles for her 'system' of property management, requiring self-improvement and the punctual payment of rent from her tenants or eviction. From 1864 until her death, she published an annual *Letter to My Fellow Workers* and by the mid-1880s — when the Church Commissioners asked her to take over some of their estates in Southwark — she was managing or 're-forming' about 3,500 tenants. In 1884 the Prince of Wales tried to get her nominated as a member of the Royal Commission on the Housing of the Working Classes, but Gladstone objected to the appointment of a woman. In the 1890s her time was spent increasingly in training enough lady rent-collectors or 'friendly visitors' to meet the demand, eventually leading to the setting up of the Women's Housing Managers Association. She was one of the pioneers of the National Trust and the Charity Organization Society. In 1909 she sat on the Royal Commission on the Poor Laws, strongly dissenting against its support for State relief schemes. Octavia Hill never married but there is evidence that she suffered from a nervous breakdown as a result of an engagement broken off when she was nearly 40.

NEVILL, Percy Bantock, (1887-1975)

Nevill was the son of Lieutenant-Colonel Charles Henry Nevill, of the 1st Surrey Rifles Territorials, a chartered accountant, living on the Ridgeway, Enfield. Educated at the Free Church, Mill Hill Public School, in 1912 Nevill joined his father's firm, Nevill, Hovey and Gardner and Co., as a junior partner. In 1943 Nevill retired completely from the firm to devote his whole time to Scouting and youth work. In 1913 he was appointed Assistant District Commissioner for Enfield; in 1918 asked to join the Scout Council. Nevill went on to become Acting District Commissioner of East London, on behalf of Roland Philipps, who was killed in action in July 1916; then he was made first Warden of Roland House (1919-1925); joined the executive com-mittee of the Boy Scouts Association in 1921; became Commissioner for Kindred Societies (1922-1951); Commissioner in Charge of the Grants Department (1938-1963); and was put in charge of the Rover Department at Headquarters (1929-1936), etc. In 1945, Nevill received the O.B.E. in recognition of his services to Scouting. Nevill married in 1926 and went to live in Reigate, Surrey, where he became associated with the 2nd Reigate Group, of which he was President until his death in 1975.

PATON, John Brown, (1830-1911)

Born near Glasgow on 17 December 1830, to the manager of a co-operative store, at 15 Paton became a school master in Gloucester, then trained to be a Minister at Springhill College, Birmingham (1846-1854), becoming a Congregational Minister in Sheffield (1854-1863); then he was for 35 years Principal of the Congregational Institute (now the Paton Congregational College) at Nottingham (1863-1898). Paton founded the Bible Reading Union in 1892 and such organizations as the Boys' League of Honour, Guilds of Courtesy and the Young Men's Brigade of Service. He died aged 81 in 1911.

PAUL, Leslie, (1905-   )

Born in Dublin, educated at the Central School until he was 15, Paul became a free-lance journalist after depressing early years working as an office boy in a warehouse in Whitechapel. In the 1930s he became the editor of *Plan*, the journal of H. G. Wells and C. E. M. Joad's Federation of Progressive Societies and Individuals. He visited Germany, Austria and the Soviet Union, writing *Co-operation in the U.S.S.R.* (1932). In 1934 he resigned as Headman of the Woodcraft Folk and was succeeded by Basil Rawson who remained President until his death in 1976. Since 1944 Paul has moved back to a strong Christian commitment and has written many books on philosophical and ethical subjects, such as *The Meaning of Human Existence* (1949). He is also the author of the Paul Report on the *Payment and Deployment of the Clergy* (1965), brought up to date in his *A Church by Daylight* (1974). Now retired, for some time Paul was Lecturer in Ethics and Social Science at the Queen's College, Birmingham. See Leslie Paul, *Angry Young Man: an autobiography* (London, 1951).

RIDGE, Dr John James, (1847-1908)

John Ridge was born in Gravesend, where his father, a well known local physician, was twice Mayor. Having won a scholarship from the City of London School to St Thomas' Hospital and practiced in Clapham, he came to Enfield in 1872 and joined the Congregational Church at Chase Side; becoming an active figure in local Liberal politics. A total abstainer, he established the British Medical Temperance Association in 1876, of which he was the first President, and was co-founder of Enfield Cottage Hospital. In his professional capacity, he was widely known from 1881 as the Enfield Medical Officer of Health.

SALMOND, Albert Louis, (-1902)

Albert Salmond, a Captain in the Derby Militia, was a coal owner and solicitor. Despite his initial appearance of 'melancholic pessimism', he proved, according to Henry Nevinson, to be 'one of the few inspired and unselfish enthusiasts I have ever known', giving unstinted service to the Battalion. Until his untimely death in 1902, from wounds received while serving as Commandant of Stormberg with his old regiment the 3rd Sherwood Foresters in South Africa, he was a mainstay of the Southwark cadets. He was the uncle of Sir William Salmond, Air Chief Marshal in the early 1930s.

SEGESSER, Felix, (1863-1930)

Felix Segesser was born in 1863 at Lucerne, Switzerland, brought to St Leonards, Hastings, and educated at St. Mary's Lodge, a local preparatory school. He trained for the priesthood at St. Columbia's College, Ushaw, Co. Durham, being ordained in 1890. He was Vice-Rector of the Diocesan Seminary at Wonersh (1890-1896); Curate at Bermondsey (1896-1905); Missionary Rector of the Church of Assumption, Deptford (1905-1916). He then left to return to St Leonards, his boyhood home, as parish priest of St Thomas of Canterbury, becoming Rural Dean of Hastings until his death, after a long illness, in 1930. See Obituaries: the *Universe,* 2 January 1931, p. 4; *Catholic Times,* 26 December 1930; the *Hastings and St. Leonards Observer,* 27 December 1930.

SETON, Ernest Thompson, (1860-1946)

Ernest Thompson Seton was born in South Shields, England, but in 1866 his family emigrated to Ontario, Canada, living as pioneers in the backwoods, teaching Seton the techniques of woodcraft and self-reliance. After studying in Toronto and London, which led to a breakdown in his health, Seton spent much of the next few years camping out in the forests of Manitoba, making a particular study of wild life. Later he travelled through North America, studied painting in Paris and settled down on a farm in New England. He became one of America's greatest naturalists and an author of animal stories for children, as well as a fine illustrator of outdoor life. See Brian Morris, 'Ernest Thompson Seton and the origins of the Woodcraft movement', *The Journal of Contemporary History,* Vol. 5, No. 2, (1970), pp. 183-194; Heinz Reichling, *Ernest Thompson Seton und die Woodcraft Bemegung in*

England (Bonn, 1937).

SMITH, Sir William Alexander, (1854-1914)

Born on 27 October 1854 near Thurso, on the coast of Caithness, Smith was the eldest of three sons of Major David Smith of the local Caithness Volunteers and the daughter of Alexander Fraser, a Glasgow merchant. His education at the Miller Institution or 'Thurso Academy' was cut short on his father's death in 1868 when the widow sold the family home and accepted her brother's offer to take William into his Glasgow home and business. For a few months in 1869 he went to a private school before going to live with his uncle and aunts in West Glasgow. In 1872 he joined the YMCA and met his future first wife, Amelia Pearson Sutherland, the daughter of a Presbyterian Chaplain to the troops at Gibraltar, but they did not get married for another twelve years. In 1874, aged 20, he first heard Moody and Sankey, joined the Free Church and also the 1st Lanarkshire Rifle Volunteers. In 1879, after a dispute with his uncle, Smith went into business himself in Glasgow, as a wholesale 'shawl dealer'. He had also become Secretary of a Sunday School Teachers' Society and a Young Men's Club attached to a new mission in North Woodside which, in 1883, provided the nucleus for the Boys' Brigade. Smith gave up his business in 1888 to become the first full-time Secretary of the rapidly expanding Boys' Brigade. His two sons by his first marriage, Stanley and Douglas, both followed him into the movement. Smith remarried in 1906 – his first wife had died in 1898 – but his second wife, Hannah Ranken Campbell, died soon after, on their return to Scotland from a visit to America. The founder of the Boys' Brigade himself died on 8 May 1914, during an executive meeting in London, after attending the annual Albert Hall BB Display.

VANE, Sir Francis Fletcher, (1861-1934)

Francis Fletcher Vane was descended from a famous aristocratic family tracing itself back to Sir Harry Vane the Younger in the seventeenth century. Vane was a contemporary of Baden-Powell's at Charterhouse in the mid-1870s, and was at the Oxford Military College from 1876 to 1879, then held various commands in the Militia and the Volunteers until in 1886 he became a Resident at Toynbee Hall. From 1886 to 1893, Vane was involved with a trading syndicate promoted by W. T. Stead and the *Pall Mall Gazette* to improve Anglo-Russian relations. During the war in South Africa, in which he served in many different capacities, Vane made himself unpopular with his fellow-officers for his indictment of the British treatment of Boer civilians

(see *Pax Britannica in South Africa,* 1905). In 1906 he contested
Burton-on-Trent unsuccessfully as a Liberal Imperialist and in 1909 he
was dismissed by Baden-Powell (q.v.) from the post of Scout Commissioner for London. He was declared a bankrupt in 1912 largely owing
to his support for both the British Boy Scouts and the Italian Scouts,
the latter founded during his frequent absences abroad. Vane was in
Dublin as a Major during the Easter 1916 Uprising and because of his
chivalric sense of honour alerted the authorities to the notorious
'Skeffington murders' of civilians by a firing squad (see *'Agin the
Governments,* 1929, chap. xv). After the First World War, he settled
in Italy until the Boy Scouts were suppressed by Mussolini in 1927 in
favour of the Balilla. Vane appears to have become reconciled with
Baden-Powell, for they were in correspondence again until a few
months before Sir Francis' death.

WESTLAKE, Ernest, (1856-1922)

Ernest Westlake was the son of a wealthy sail-cloth manufacturer and
devout Quaker of East Mills in the Hampshire Avon valley. Brought
up in an atmosphere of narrow puritanism, he showed no aptitude for
his father's business and decided to devote himself to scientific study,
training as a geologist under Huxley and Tyndal at University College,
London. Living as rather a scholarly recluse until his unexpected
marriage in 1891, the death of his wife in 1900 came as a great blow
to him. In 1904 while on a cycling holiday in France with his daughter
and her governess, he made the exciting discovery of a large number of
pre-historic stone weapons and implements at Aurillac in the Cantal.
In 1908 a growing interest in anthropology led him to Tasmania where
he found similar stone implements. Westlake became a pioneering
Fellow of the Anthropological Institute which led to his interest in
the theory of 'recapitulation'. A founder of the Order of Woodcraft
Chivalry, he was killed in a car accident in 1922. See William van der
Eyken and Barry Turner, *Adventures in Education* (London, 1969),
'The Forest School: 1929-1938', pp. 125 44.